Like the dandelion, the child...

-is full of potential
-is carried by the winds that influence his life
-can be rooted and grounded in the soil of love
-digs deeply and steadily toward what enlightens him
-can be tenacious, holding onto life with all he's got
-can wither if he's uprooted,
 or if the soil does not provide nutrients
-can be resilient, bouncing back from hardship
-can grow to spread seeds of himself, his ideas, near
 and far
-must bloom to become all he's meant to be
-sometimes looks like a weed, but is really a flower.

There is an adage:
"Children need roots to grow and wings to fly."
The dandelion has both.

Karyn Henley

CHILD-SENSITIVE TEACHING™

Helping children grow a living faith in a loving God

by

Karyn Henley

Child Sensitive Communication, LLC

CHILD-SENSITIVE TEACHING:
Helping children grow a living faith in a loving God
by Karyn Henley

Originally published: Nashville, Tenn.: Allen Thomas Pub., 1994.
Second publication: Cincinnati, Ohio: Standard Pub., 1997
Third publication: Nashville, TN: Child Sensitive Communication, LLC, 2002

This 2008 REVISED AND UPDATED edition (4th) published by:

Child Sensitive Communication, LLC
POB 40269
Nashville, TN 37204-0269
1-888-573-3953 (toll-free U.S.)
www.KarynHenley.com

Cover design: Ralph Henley
Illustrations: Joe Stites
Layout: Kristi West

ISBN 13: 978-1-933803-48-7
ISBN 10:   1-933803-48-7

Contents

Communication in the Classroom

The Growing Teacher

Introduction

The sign on the wall beside the Sunday school classroom said,
"Teachers are invited guests.
Parents are the real teachers."
Whether you are the parent or the classroom teacher, the challenge remains the same: How do we guide our children into a strong and lasting relationship with God our Father, with His Son, Jesus, and with His Holy Spirit? The question is all about communication. How can we communicate most effectively?

Teaching is not just dispensing information, it's touching lives. It's not just managing a classroom or a household, it's uncovering the path to life. It's throwing open the doors to God's kingdom and saying, "Have you met my Father? Have you met His Son? Let me introduce you and then, let's both get to know Him better."

When it comes to communication, there are many factors for a teacher to think about: curricula, methods, materials, facilities, schedule, co-workers, classroom management techniques. All of these are important and are covered in this book. But nothing is as important as the child and your relationship with him or her. Your relationship with the child will affect all the other factors and will determine the effectiveness of your communication.

So while *Child-Sensitive Teaching* focuses on understanding the child and his needs, it also deals with preparing your heart and mind to communicate with children. It also suggests practical methods and techniques to support your communication skills.

I pray that God will go far beyond these black words on white pages. I pray that God will guide you deeper into relationship with Him and bring to your mind ways to communicate His heart to the specific children you work with each week. I pray that *Child-Sensitive Teaching* will be a springboard for your own God-given vision and creativity.

The Growing
CHILD

Chapter 1

The Child's-Eye View

What's it Like to be a Child?

"Life is hard. You have to go potty even when you don't want to."
-3 year old

When I held my first grandson in my arms, something amazing happened. As I looked at his tiny face, I saw in him not only the infant, but the four-year-old, the eight-year-old, the fourteen-year-old, the youth, and the man. From raising my own sons, I knew how quickly the time passes. Here, cradled in my arms, was a man.

In these first few chapters, we are preparing to cross a wide span of time and look closely at each developmental stage. If you work with older children or youth, you may be tempted to skip the chapters that deal with younger kids. If you work with preschoolers, you may be tempted to skip the information about older children. But I encourage you to stay with us for the entire ride. I want you to see the full scope of faith and moral development. Why?

1. Seeing the big picture will help you understand children better. It's very easy to get tunnel vision and see a child as simply a four-year-old or a ten-year-old instead of a whole, developing person. You will be a better parent and/or teacher by being aware of the growth process, knowing the previous stage, anticipating the coming stage.

2. Seeing the big picture will prepare you to understand a major point I will be emphasizing later, once you have an understanding of developmental stages.

3. If you are a teacher, seeing the big picture will help you see yourself as part of a team addressing the needs of children at different stages, contributing to the healthy development of the child as a whole person.

We are going to start with a look at young children. If you have spent time with preschoolers, you know they often say and do wonderful things that give us a peek into their minds. I used to write down some of the insights my children, now grown, gave me when they were preschoolers. My older son, Raygan, called his echo his "hide and seek voice." A nest was a "bird pocket." Wigs were "put on hairs." A life jacket was a "splashing coat."

While putting on his underpants one day, Raygan began to "read" the tag: "And I will dwell in the house of the Lord forever," he said. When he bit off more peanut butter and jelly sandwich than he could chew, he spit out the whole mouthful and said, "I need another one. This one is dead."

My younger son, Heath, was just as clever. He called his head bone his "skull-a-ton." One day he said, "I'm gonna' buy me some new legs. These legs hurt in my flip-flops." Heath saved everything in the refrigerator (which he called the "fwizwator"). He even stored pennies and rocks in the fridge.

We often laugh at things children say and do. Sometimes we cry over what they say and do! But if you want to work with children, no matter their age, watching and listening to them is very important. That's because watching and listening to children gives you clues about how they think. You learn what they understand and what they don't understand. When you know how they think and what they understand, you can communicate better with them.

Children amaze us. Sometimes we stand back, shaking our heads. "This child is off in a world of his own," we say. And that's true. He is.

Do you remember what it was like to be a child? Do you remember what it was like to be misunderstood? What was it like to misunderstand? What was it like to need to wiggle? What was it like to feel like dancing? What was it like to be laughed at? What was it like to have to wait? What was it like to watch tiny things and to wonder?

As I've studied the art and craft of writing for children, I've learned that if I want to impact children in a significant way, I must reach into myself and touch my own childhood. I have to see through the eyes of the child in me and to write to make that child laugh or cry or gasp or giggle.

> When you work with children, it is critically important to remember what it was like to be a child.

When you work with children, it is critically important to remember what it was like to be a child. Of course, it may not be easy to look back at your childhood. Some childhoods do not make good memories. Some are full of pain, rejection, abuse and hurt. But even so, there is good reason to remember your past. The good reason is the children who are hurting today. These are some of the same children you will be working with as you teach.

Jesus told Peter, "Simon, Satan has asked to sift you as wheat. But I have prayed for you, Simon, that your faith may not fail. **And when you have turned back, strengthen your brothers**" (Luke 22:32, emphasis mine). Do you feel like you were sifted in childhood? Strengthen your little brothers and sisters. Because you understand. Paul wrote, "God… comforts us in all our troubles so that we can comfort those in any trouble with the comfort we ourselves have received from God" (2 Corinthians 1:3, 4).

Paul knew hardship from experience. Jesus did too, having been "tempted in every way, just as we are… Let us then approach the throne of grace with confidence, so that we may receive mercy and find grace to help us in our time of need" (Hebrews 4:15, 16). Jesus wasn't human for nothing. He knows what it's like to get angry. He knows what it's like to be concerned. He know how it feels to be disappointed and betrayed. He knows what it's like to laugh and cry. He knows what it feels like to be weary. Or to be misunderstood. Or to be laughed at. He knows what it's like to win and to lose.

As adults, we know these things too. We know what it's like to be a child. We've been there. We weren't kids for nothing. So children should be able to "receive mercy" from us. They should be able to find from us "grace to help . . . in time of need."

A Child's World

Let's look at the world from a child's-eye view. Let's try to remember what it was like.

1. A child views the world with his own logic.

David Elkind says, "Children are most like us in feeling, least like us in thinking."[1] Children are relatively new in the world. They try to make sense of the world the best they can. They respond in ways that are logical to them. But many times, their logic stems from their imagination. All it takes is listening to a child to see that his thoughts are not like yours. In the next few chapters, we'll see more about why this is true.

Do you want to communicate well with children? Then listen to them. Hear how they think. Consider their logic.

One of my sons called pants legs "leg sleeves." Logical, isn't it? When he was three, he was fascinated by my sewing scissors. They were very sharp, so I kept them in a plastic sheath when he was around. One day as he was looking at the scissors in their sheath, he asked, "Can it sizz?" Washers wash, clippers clip, scissors must sizz. Of course. It makes perfect sense.

2. A child's world is full of possibilities.

In the 1940's, Shinichi Suzuki, a violinist from Japan, developed a method of teaching young children how to play musical instruments. He said, "The potential of every child is unlimited." Another Japanese teacher, also named Suzuki, said, "In the beginner's mind there are many possibilities; in the expert's mind there are few."[2] Children believe that almost anything is possible. They will often say, "I can do it" when we have great doubts about whether they really can or not.

I remember telling my mother that I could carry a pie from the car to the house. The pie didn't make it. Thanks to Mother's grace, I did. Thinking anything is possible sometimes gets children into trouble. But it is also one of the motivators that helps children learn and accomplish difficult tasks.

3. A child's world is a mixture of fantasy and reality.

Thinking anything is possible stems in part from a child's active imagination. Until a child is about five years old, she has a hard time distinguishing fantasy from reality. As far as she's concerned, Big Bird is a real friend of hers. Curious George can come over and play in the back yard. At night when everyone is asleep, the tea cups and saucers come out of the cupboards to sing and dance like they do in Disney movies. Animals can talk and action figures can have real adventures.

One day I was getting ready to run some errands. My preschool son asked, "Mommy, will you do me a favorite? Will you drive by the river and get a duck and bring him home? And if you see a hippopotamus and an elephant, let them ride with you."

Before I had children, I taught at a private preschool in the Los Angeles area. One day we were preparing to grill hot dogs outside. A teacher had begun to light the coals in the grill. One little boy watched intently. Then, pointing to the charcoal, he asked, "Are those gonna' turn into hot dogs?" He was watching to see if something magic was going to happen.

Psychologists know that people respond to situations based on their perception of reality, not based on reality itself. A child's world is so steeped in imagination that her reactions are often based on fantasy. So children tend to respond more strongly than we do, expressing feelings that are overly fearful, extremely worried, or extra excited. Throughout childhood, all the way through adolescence, the child's response level and ours may be very different.

4. A child's world is less inhibited than an adult's.

When a child is born, he is completely egocentric. He doesn't worry about what people are going to think of him. He doesn't worry about social conventions or about what's proper in front of others. He is very uninhibited. More than one preschool teacher has heard family secrets blurted out in class.

The younger the child, the less inhibited he tends to be. If young children don't know a word to describe something, they're not inhibited. They just make up a word. One four-year-old said, "I got cookie stuck in the top of my mouth, so I took my tongue and thwooshed it out."

I stood in line at the post office recently, passing the time by watching a little girl who was about 18 months old. Everyone else was watching her too. While her mother waited in line, the little girl climbed on top of and into everything. She pulled large mailing envelopes out of their display and tugged on the ropes that kept the rest of us in line. This little one was full of energy and was using as much of it as her mom would allow.

When it was time for the little girl to leave, she waved good-bye to everyone in line. All of us waved back, except for one man. He was engrossed in his piece of mail. Undaunted and uninhibited, this little girl walked right up to him and waved at his face.

5. A child's world is full of curiosities.

A child is very aware that there are lots of things she does not know, and she has a natural curiosity to find out about them. If she doesn't burn out on learning, that desire to discover can stay with her into adulthood.

Four- and five-year-olds are at a prime time in their lives for discovering and learning about their world. At this age, they ask lots of questions. I went on a field trip with my four-year-old class one day. As we rode along, I pointed out interesting sights to the little boy who sat beside me on the bus. When I spied a flat bed truck carrying an old house, I said, "Look at that truck moving a house."

My little friend gazed at the sight in awe, then asked, "Where are the roots?"

6. A child's world is often overwhelming.

There's a lot about the adult world that children don't understand. So children may have fears that seem unreasonable to adults. My son wanted the window shades closed when it was dark, "so the night won't come in."

The physical scale of a child's world is much bigger to him than our world is to us. Do you remember what it was like to sit in chairs when your feet wouldn't touch the floor? Do you remember not being able to see the top of the kitchen counter? Do you remember standing in a group of grown-ups and looking them squarely in the belt?

Imagine how it would feel if stairs were proportioned to you the way they are to a child. How high would you have to step? Think of the energy it would take to go up a flight of stairs if they were almost knee high to you. A child spends much of his time getting around, over, past or through the physical obstacles that surround him every day.

But the physical world isn't the only thing that's overwhelming. Along with the rest of us, the child is bombarded every day by all sorts of things vying for his attention. The average American is confronted with 3,000 advertisements a day. That's 1,095,000 ads a year. By the time a child is 15, he's seen more than 16,425,000 ads.[3] Each ad tries to be more lively or colorful, louder or brighter in the competition over who can catch the public's attention.

One spring, our symphony gave a children's concert that took us on a tour of music from the beginning of time up to the last years of the 20th century. The first "music" we heard was from nature: a brook gurgling, birds singing, wind stirring leaves in the trees, a dog barking.

As each period of music went by, there were more and more instruments, more and more sounds. It progressed until we heard avant garde music, a cacophony of machine and traffic sounds accompanied by instruments. The symphony conductor made the comment that in these days, we learn to block out sounds. All day, we shut out peripheral sound in order to focus on what we're doing.

Is this why I can stand three feet from a child, call his name and get no response? Maybe he is shutting out sound so he can focus and concentrate on what he's doing.

7. A child's world is "now."

We adults often talk about how fast time passes. Every year seems to pass faster and faster. I was talking about this to one of my sons when he was sixteen. He pointed out, "A year *is* shorter to an adult. Just think about it. To a six-year-old, a year is one-sixth of his entire life. To a forty-six-year-old, a year is only one-forty-sixth of his entire life. It's shorter as you get older."

Bypassing those philosophical issues, the reality is that young children do not have the mental capacity to comprehend the flow of time. To a young child, "long ago" was yesterday at Grandma's house. You can tell her, "In two weeks, it will be your birthday," but she'll wake up tomorrow and ask, "Is it my birthday yet?" Christmas may be "just around the corner," but that seems like an eternity to a young child. A few years ago, a family that lives in our neighborhood left early in the morning to drive across country to Grandma's for a family vacation. The mom tried to explain to their preschooler that they had a long drive ahead of them. She said, "We won't get there until after we've eaten breakfast, lunch, and dinner. After dinner, we'll get there." Her preschool son said, "Then let's eat dinner now."

The ability to comprehend the flow of time does not develop until children are between six and eight years old. Even then, they live very much in the present. Getting a handle on the flow of time develops bit by bit and increases with the brain growth that occurs in adolescence.

8. A child's world is self-focused.

Children are not born thinking of others. The younger the child, the more naturally self-centered he is. If a baby is cold or hungry or wet or uncomfortable, he usually communicates it immediately. The world revolves around him. He knows nothing else.

As the child grows, he begins to interact with more and more of the world around him. He works hard to find out how he affects his world. Gradually he begins to see other people's needs. But voluntarily putting others first demands a high level of maturity. We will see that this maturity develops as the child's own needs are met. When a child's needs are met, he becomes free to reach out and help meet the needs of other people.

Why Study Childhood?

Part of being child-sensitive is trying to see what the world feels like from the child's perspective. That information is valuable to us, because it helps us see the child's needs more clearly. It helps us respect the child. It helps us communicate more effectively.

As we've seen, one way to know the child's viewpoint is to remember what it was like to be a child. Another way is to watch children and listen to them. A third way is to learn from people who have studied children. We will be learning from some of these experts in the following pages.

One of these experts is Robert Coles, a professor of psychiatry and medical humanities at Harvard Medical School. Dr. Coles received a Pulitzer prize for his five-volume **Children of Crisis** series. He has spent over thirty years listening to children. In an interview about children, he said, "They offer us a chance to see a good part of what we are: human beings struggling to figure out what this world means." Coles urges us to "regard children as fellow human beings yet to be constricted and constrained the way that some of us have been as we have made the various compromises that are called growing up."

He says, "The point is not to romanticize children but to understand the... perspective they have... They are new on the block, so to speak. As a consequence they have a certain kind of openness of mind and heart."[4]

There's another reason for trying to see the world from a child's viewpoint. Jesus said, "Unless you change and become like little children, you will never enter the kingdom of heaven" (Matthew 18:3). If for no other reason than this, childhood is worth a good, long look.

In God's Kingdom, we are all children of the Father. So, as it happens, we are children teaching children. We can all rejoice to hear him say, "Let the little children come to me... for the kingdom of God belongs to such as these" (Mark 10:14).

Chapter 2

S.O.S. BEAR
The Needs of Childhood

The sun was shining as a four-year old
and his mother went into K-Mart.
While they were shopping,
dark clouds gathered and covered the sun.
It was cloudy and dark
by the time the boy and his mom left the store.
"Where did God go?" asked the boy.
"He was here a minute ago."

Tuned-in Adults

One of our goals as teachers and parents is to help children reach a level of maturity at which they put others first. They help. They share. They give. Our hope is that they will serve others because they choose to, not because they're forced to.

At first glance, it might seem that focusing on meeting a child's needs gives too much attention to the child. Won't that keep him centered on himself? No. In fact, just the opposite is true. The child whose needs are met can focus on other people, instead of on his own unfulfilled needs. He doesn't have to spend time trying to get his own needs met.

We are talking about *needs* now, not *wants*. It's possible that what a child wants is also what he needs. But it's quite possible that what he wants is not at all what he needs. That's why one of his greatest needs is adults who are tuned in to him and can help him make right choices. These adults will not cater to his every want, but will try to provide for his needs.

Our human tendency is to treat others the way we've been treated. So when we meet a child's needs, we model for him how to help others. If we treat a child with respect, he is more likely to treat others with respect. This is the way God deals with us. "We love because he first loved us" (1 John 4:19).

Children's Needs
So what are the needs of children?

1. Security

Every child needs a place where he can feel safe and secure. First of all, he needs physical safety. Oftentimes, we protect children from real dangers that they are not even aware of. At other times, children are afraid and we are not. Some of the most common fears of preschool children are imaginary: ghosts, monsters, and things lurking in the dark. But between the ages of seven and twelve, imagined fears are replaced by fears of bodily injury and natural disaster. The greatest fears at this stage are real: drive-by shootings, kidnappers, gangs, and drugs. Even among adolescents, the top fears are related to death and physical danger.[1]

But children also need to feel safe from emotional attack. One of the biggest fears of all people, including children, is the fear of rejection, criticism, and mockery. Whatever their fears, kids need to feel safe around us. Whether our children are young or almost grown, if we can have age-appropriate rules, be consistent, and maintain fairly predictable schedules and routines, we will contribute a great deal toward helping kids feel secure.

2. Optimism

Ranking close to the fear of rejection is the fear of failure. The child who is afraid to fail is the child who stops trying. Someone may have told him that he'll never make it. Or that he'll never be good enough. And he believed them. The fear of failure paralyzes people.

Optimism helps to combat the fear of failure. Optimism believes things are going to work out for the best. It helps us keep going when things get tough. It's the light at the end of the tunnel. It encourages us to see failures and hardships as stepping stones instead of stumbling blocks. Children need our optimism. They need us to encourage them so that when life hands them a lemon, as the old saying goes, they can "make lemonade."

They need adults who have a kind sense of humor, adults who can laugh at their own mistakes and look forward to a bright future. Solomon wrote, "Though a righteous man falls seven times, he rises again" (Proverbs 24:16). God's people have every reason to be optimistic. "All things work together for good for them that love God" (Romans 8:28, KJV).

3. Significance

All people need to feel that they are important to someone. Children are no different. What makes you feel significant? Someone acknowledges your presence, welcomes you, spends time with you, listens to you, values your work and your efforts, asks you to join them in their work and play. When adults notice children, speak to them, listen to them, call them by their names, children feel significant.

People also feel significant when they feel needed. When you are able to help someone else, to serve them, to do tasks that are productive and meaningful, you feel significant. This is true of children, too. As they grow and learn to do more on their own, they feel competent and significant.

Why is feeling significant so important? As one mother said, "When people feel worthless, they act worthless." But when people feel significant, they act as if what they do will be significant. They believe what they do and say will make a difference. That motivates them to be more responsible. They don't want to jeopardize their self-respect or the respect that others have for them.

So check your attitude toward children. Do you feel like they are a nuisance? Are they "in the way"? Or are they a treasure to you? Are you glad to get rid of them? Or are you sorry to see them go? Your attitude will be communicated to children, even if you don't say it in words.

"Let the little children come to me," said Jesus (Matthew 19:14). If we are to grow to be like Jesus, we will grow in kindness and love toward children.

4. Belonging

Closely linked to significance is belonging. Everyone needs to feel like they belong somewhere. They need to feel like they fit, like they are welcome. Belonging has to do with finding a place in the group.

What are some important groups for children? Family. Classmates. Neighbors and other friends. Club members and even co-workers. How do these groups give a child a sense of belonging? They include him in what they do. They encourage him to contribute to discussions. They listen and value his input. They give him a role to play that directly benefits the group, so he can see that what he does enables the group to function, even to survive.

These roles include jobs or chores. In the classroom and in families, children should have age-appropriate jobs, tasks that they can accomplish successfully. Children need to feel needed.

5. Exploration

Children need freedom to explore. This does not mean they should be left completely to themselves, unsupervised, with no limits. It simply means they need some unstructured, non-directed, free time.

Time is a precious commodity. We spend much of it running here and there. We fill time with music lessons, dance lessons, gymnastics, ball practices and games. While those activities can be fun, they can also deprive a child of much-needed blocks of free time. A child needs time to think on his own, to watch ants, smell clover, taste honeysuckle, blow dandelion seeds. He needs time to work through boredom and move into creativity.

That means children need to have access to materials that encourage them to exercise their curiosity safely, to explore, to discover. Having a variety of safe, interesting material available encourages children to explore. The adult then makes himself available as a resource person to help the child as needed. But the adult does not direct the activity or intervene in the activity unless it's necessary.

6. Appreciation of Childhood

Children need people who appreciate the fact that they're children. Our society pressures kids to grow up quickly. But God made children to grow and mature according to a general pattern, not only physically, but mentally, emotionally and spiritually as well. No amount of pushing and pressuring can change that. It's a process.

We can manipulate kids by getting them to dress like grown-ups and talk with grown-up words, but that doesn't mean they are more grown up. Their appearance and speech may fool some people, but an underlying immaturity will surface. The outward signs will be out of step with the inner, God-given growth pattern.

How can we show children that we appreciate their age? How do we show that we accept them on their level? We provide material they can use and activities they can do successfully. We choose child-sized furniture and equipment for our classrooms. We make our teaching relevant to their age level and interests.

This same principle holds true for children who have special needs. We accept them as they are. If the child is in a wheelchair, we provide activities he can do successfully. If a child is color blind, we avoid color matching activities for him. If he is a poor reader, we avoid asking him to read the Bible passage out loud. Instead, we help these children accomplish tasks in areas where they can succeed.

7. Relationship

Relationship in itself is neither positive or negative. The link between two things could be strong or weak, good or bad. What children want and need are good, strong relationships with wise, caring adults.

In our society, generational links of relationship have broken down. God originally made the older to teach and train the younger. When the world began, and for thousands of years after that, families were intergenerational groups that worked and played together. Children lived not only among parents and siblings, but also grandparents, great-grandparents, aunts and uncles. The older generations were revered for their experienced, wise counsel.

Our present day culture centers around youth. People are separated into age-segregated peer groups that often look down their noses at the younger and mistrust and ridicule the older. But for children, a good, warm relationship with a caring adult can be a foundation for growth in every area of development. As we will see, this type of relationship is a critical component in building faith and moral values.

The One Who Meets All Needs

Security
Optimism
Significance

Belonging
Exploration
Appreciation of Childhood
Relationship

As an acrostic, these words spell "S.O.S BEAR." When a child's needs have not been met, very often he will send an S.O.S. signal by his behavior. (We will look specifically at behavior in a later chapter.) Of course, only God can completely satisfy all the child's needs. So sensitive adults act as guides to lead the child to his Heavenly Father, who can and will meet every need, although perhaps not according to our agenda or on our timetable. But God loves perfectly, and Perfect Love is faithful.

26

Our own needs are very similar to those of the child. So we teachers and parents continue to rely on God to meet our needs, too. God keeps us **secure** in His love. We can be **optimistic**, because He is in control and works out His plans for our good and His glory. We are **significant** to him, counting our worth by the great price He paid for us. Now we **belong** to God the Creator as His precious children. He has given us a whole world of sensory experiences and ideas to **explore**, including His own rich, limitless store of wisdom and knowledge. He accepts and **appreciates** each of us individually right where we are in our development. And He has invited us to enter into an intimate **relationship** with Him. He delights in our relationship and gives us opportunity daily to fall deeper in love with Him.

God's love is our greatest treasure. As we share this treasure, it multiplies like the loaves and fish. Let's continue to look for the best way to share it.

Chapter 3

The House That Faith Built

Faith Development

*"When Jesus comes again,
we will all hold onto kites,
and the wind will blow and blow
and blow us up to Heaven."*

- 4 year old

Seekers

The year Naomi was in my four-year-old class, I probably learned more from her than she learned from me. She was petite, with an olive complexion, dark straight hair, and deep brown, thoughtful eyes. She loved Jesus and was ready to share him with her friends.

In group time one night, Kara announced that her tummy hurt. Before I had time to say, "Let's pray for Kara," Naomi had already moved beside Kara. She had placed her hands on Kara's arm and was praying.

I have not seen many children who were as spiritually sensitive as Naomi. But we need not be fooled. Children are spiritual beings, just as adults are. They have deep, important questions and thoughts. They are often more ready to express a simple, matter-of-fact faith in Jesus than we adults who have become skeptical about anything we can't experience with our five senses.

Robert Coles, in his book, The *Spiritual Life of Children*, says that the research and writing of that book was "a project that, finally, helped me see children as seekers, as young pilgrims well aware that life is a finite journey and as anxious to make sense of it as those of us who are farther along in the time allotted us."[1]

Children are busy creatures, working every day to find their place in the world. A child works at becoming her own person, discovering who she is. She works at establishing her individual identity. She works at growing physically, mentally, emotionally, and spiritually.

We have an important role to play in helping children become all God made them to be. Our goal is for our children to become independent in their dependence on God. We want them, of their own will, to seek God and establish an eternity-long relationship with Him.

Growing Up in Our Salvation

The apostle Peter encouraged us to "grow up in our salvation" (1 Peter 2:1-3). In a sense, salvation is like the shoes or shirt we buy a size too large, knowing our child will "grow into it." We receive our salvation from Jesus. We are saved. Period. The work has been done. But salvation is much too big for us. Thanks to God's grace, we have the rest of our lives to "grow into it."

Since we work with children, it's important to know about the growth process. It's important for us to see where children have been and where they are going. We cannot transfer our faith to them by osmosis, but we can help them "prepare Him room," as the Christmas song says.

At some point, belief in the facts about Jesus must become faith in Jesus. The lifestyle of Christianity must become life in Jesus. Head knowledge must become heart knowledge. Our wills must be submitted to His will. Allegiance to "a church" and a set of doctrines must become subordinate to total surrender to Jesus. We must come to know Him as our best friend, our Master, our Lord.

Some people accept Jesus' Lordship earlier than others. Young children can be very sensitive to what Jesus has done for them and to how God wants them to respond. Others may not respond until they are teenagers or young adults. In either case, their response can be deep and life-changing. Whether people are young or old when they come into God's kingdom, their faith should continue to develop as they "grow up in salvation."

In leading people to Jesus, our place is never to manipulate them. Our job is:

- to introduce them to God and His saving grace
- to feed and nurture their spirits
- to be sensitive to their readiness
- to provide opportunities for them to express their faith as it grows, including asking Jesus to be their Lord and Savior.

We must not push for what we would like to see happen. Instead, we must wait on God and give Him room and time to work as He wills. We have the privilege of watching God work in the lives of children, so their "faith might not rest on men's wisdom, but on God's power" (1 Corinthians 2:5).

See How They Grow

In the following chapters, we'll use Erik Erikson's developmental tasks[2] to delineate stages of growth, because his "tasks" have underlying spiritual significance. In each stage, we will also look at faith development as researched by James Fowler[3]. We'll look at moral development through the research of Lawrence Kohlberg[4], Dr. Thomas Lickona[5] and Dr. William Sears[6]. We'll also see how mental development affects each stage by looking at the research of Jean Piaget[7] and Howard Gardner[8]. (I footnote them here, but not in every subsequent reference in order to avoid cluttering the remaining text with numerals.)

Two caveats:

1. No researcher has a complete understanding of their area of research. My references to some of their specific findings does not mean I completely agree with all their theories. Research in all these areas is ongoing, and other researchers may have different theories. I refer to selected, specific information from these particular sources, because the information rings true from my experience and has obvious practical applications that I find extremely helpful to me as a teacher and parent.

2. Developmental stages are true in a general sense. No one is a statistic, and not everyone follows the growth pattern exactly. Some children develop more quickly, some more slowly. Still, everyone follows the same general blueprint.

Growing Faith

Growing faith is a bit like building a house. In this case, each house is a temple in which the living God desires to dwell: "Do you not know that your body is a temple of the Holy Spirit, who is in you, whom you have received from God?" wrote Paul (1 Corinthians 6:19). As David said, "the Temple . . . is not just another building – it is for the Lord God himself!" (1 Chronicles 29:1).

Each child we teach, each temple we help build, is unique. Think of Noah, Moses, David, Daniel, Mary, Peter, Paul. Each one had a deep faith in God, a faith on which their lives were founded. But they were very different individuals. God called and used each of them in very different ways.

The following study shows us the structural framework for faith, which is built in stages as children develop. One thing this study does *not* show us is the point at which head-knowledge changes into a personal walk, when acceptance of a set of beliefs (a taken-for-granted faith) changes into abandoned trust in the Lord Jesus and dedication to His will. However, most people who have given their lives to Jesus have done it between the ages of four and fourteen.[8] A careful look at faith development in the following chapters will indicate why that's true.

What must a child know to come to God? What must any person believe to please God? 1) That He exists. 2) That He rewards those who earnestly seek Him. "Without faith it is impossible to please God, because anyone who comes to him must believe that he exists and that he rewards those who earnestly seek him" (Hebrews 11:6). Children are natural seekers. They just need us to point the way.

Realizing that Abraham believed before he ever understood has helped me in my own growing faith. God commended

Abraham for his faith, not for his understanding (Hebrews 11). But Abraham trusted because he first had a relationship.

At the seaside, Jesus called Peter, Andrew, James, and John to, "Follow me." And they did (Matthew 4:18-22). Jesus never asked them to understand. He did ask for their trust. They knew enough about Jesus and had enough or a relationship with Him that they were willing to risk their future on His leadership.

On the hillside, Jesus told His disciples to pass five loaves and two fish to 5,000 people (Matthew 14:15-21). He didn't explain it. He just asked them to trust. Their trust that day grew out of the relationship they already had with Jesus.

On the lake, Jesus told Peter to throw his fish nets into the water, although Peter had fished all night long without catching anything (Luke 5:4-6). Jesus didn't expect Peter to understand. He expected Peter to trust. Peter's relationship with Jesus was such that he was willing to trust.

As long as we live, no matter how smart we get, there will always be more of God to understand. As David said, "His greatness no one can fathom" (Psalm 145:3) So how much does a child have to understand to come to God? Not much. It begins with the child's willingness, the desires of her heart, her soul looking to God – and it grows from there. Because, as we will see, faith is not an act, it's a process.

Chapter 4

A Foundation for Faith

Faith and the Infant

From a sign posted at the church nursery door:

"We shall not all sleep,
but we shall all be changed."
1 Corinthians 15:51

The Task and the Strength

According to Erikson, there is a task that corresponds with each stage of development. In infancy, the task is to develop either TRUST, at the positive end of the scale, or MISTRUST, at the negative end. Since life is a mixture of positive and negative, there is conflict in each stage. If the positive side dominates, there emerges what Erikson called a "strength." The formation of these strengths are crucial to leading a healthy life. In the stage of infancy, when TRUST develops, the strength of HOPE emerges in the child.

What does this have to do with faith development? First of all, TRUST is a spiritual concept. God asks us to trust him. It is not easy to trust a God we can't see if we can't trust people we can see. Erikson himself said, "Out of the conflict between TRUST and MISTRUST, the infant develops HOPE which is the earliest form of what gradually becomes FAITH in adults."

So our role with infants is to instill in them a sense of trust. How do we do that? It's really very simple. We take care of their needs. The infant comes into the world completely dependent on others for his care. Our interaction with him either communicates to him that he can trust us, or it brings about a sense of mistrust.

So when the infant is hungry, we feed him. When he's cold, we wrap him in a blanket. When his diaper is wet, we put a clean diaper on him. He learns that he can trust us to take care of him. When he TRUSTS us, he has HOPE. Hope seems to be a very abstract concept for such young children. In order to make it specific and practical, let's think about hope as it relates to you, the adult, for a moment. Then we'll bring it back and apply it to the infant.

You have needs. You have seen how God meets your needs and the needs of others. So you TRUST Him. When you TRUST Him, He continues to confirm Himself to you by taking care of you in a variety of ways. Your relationship with God and your experience of His love and care give you HOPE: HOPE that your needs will be met, HOPE that even when your situation looks bleak, there's a light at the end of the tunnel. Everything will work out all right, because there's someone taking care of you. "Now FAITH is being sure of what we HOPE for..." (Hebrews 11:1).

Now let's apply this to the infant. If his caregivers are taking care of his needs, he learns he can trust them. When he trusts, he has hope that, no matter how uncomfortable he may be at any given moment (hungry or wet or cold), everything will be all right, because there's someone here whom he can trust to take care of him.

Faith in Infancy

Paul wrote to Timothy, "...from infancy you have known the holy Scriptures" (2 Timothy 3:15). As we saw in the previous section, infancy is where faith can begin to develop. Paul refers to Timothy's mother and grandmother who were believers before Timothy was born. So they obviously began early to guide Timothy into a trusting relationship with God.

Fowler says that infancy is a stage of "Undifferentiated Faith." According to Fowler, this means that the beginnings of trust, courage, hope and love are mixed together into one feeling: good. They are not experienced as separate feelings. In simple terms, the infant feels a basic sense of good and bad, pain and pleasure.

Fowler also says, "The strength of trust, autonomy, hope and courage (or their opposites) developed in this phase underlie (or threaten to undermine) all that comes later in the faith development." Are you important if you teach infants? Yes! Can you as a parent or teacher help infants learn anything spiritually significant? Yes. You can help them trust. You can plant the seeds of faith.

In addition to taking care of an infant's needs, there are other ways to introduce infants to God. These methods are simple, but they are important and appropriate to the infant's developmental level. First, because infants learn through their five senses, we point out God's creation as it relates to their immediate sensory experiences. In other words, when the infant eats a banana, we say, "God made the banana." When he smells a flower, we say, "God made the flower." When he feels the rain sprinkle down on him, we say, "God made the rain." At first, the infant does not know the word "God," but he sees, smells, touches, tastes and hears the world God made. So we begin to make the connection for him. We are introducing him to God.

We do a similar thing in order to teach about God's care and love. When the infant is cold, we wrap a warm blanket around him, or we put a sweater on him. We say, "I'm taking care of you. God takes care of you." When we rock the infant in a peaceful moment, we say, "I love you. God loves you." The infant does not know abstractions "God" or "care" or "love," but he does know the feelings he's having at those moments, feelings of being loved and cared for. So we make the connection for him. We are introducing him to God.

What's Going on in the Infant's Mind?

Since we are created in God's image, we are born with intellect. We've been made with certain built-in capabilities like creativity, exploration and discovery, the drive to communicate, laughter, personality and temperament. Researchers who don't believe in God are still trying to determine how these can be present in babies.

An infant is not a completely blank slate when he's born. But he has a lot to learn. Where is he in mental ability? How does his mind develop?

An infant's world is very tangible. It consists of what he sees, hears, smells, touches and tastes. Everything is new. Everything is being discovered. Piaget labeled this time a "sensorimotor" stage. That means infants are using their senses to learn about the world around them. Their motor skills are also developing, and infants use these skills to help them discover.

But there are other ways in which the infant is learning. Infants are fascinated by faces. This is one clue that points to the fact that infants want interaction with other people. In these interactions, their communication skills grow.

An infant's learning is also affected by his personality and temperament. Then, too, his culture affects how he learns. And he is born into a specific, unique family situation, which affects his learning as well.

Developing Morality

According to Piaget, the infant is in a premoral position. That simply means that the infant is not yet making conscious moral choices. Deuteronomy 1 shows Moses addressing God's people, reminding them that they refused to go into the Promised Land as God had instructed. Moses says, "Your children who do not yet know good from bad – they will enter the land" (Deuteronomy 1:39). Isaiah also mentions this premoral stage:

"Before the boy knows enough to reject the wrong and choose the right, the land… will be laid waste" (Isaiah 7:16).

The infant is, of course, born with a tendency to sin. We know this, because the infant is born completely self-centered, choosing his desires over the needs of others. He thinks the world revolves around him. In fact, at first the infant perceives even Mom and Dad to be an extension of himself. As far as morality goes, this is definitely square one.

So how does morality grow? We adults are an important key. The infant is aware of feeling comfort and discomfort, pain and pleasure, and even more important, acceptance and rejection. When an infant feels accepted, he is on the way to accepting and respecting others. Conversely, when an infant feels rejected, he is on the way to rejecting others. This is a basic truth of God's Kingdom: "We love because he (God) first loved us" (1 John 4:19). We respect because God first respected us. In the same way, our children love because we first loved them. They respect because we first respected them. Why is this important? Because respect for others is the foundation of morality.

Of course, the infant depends on outward cues to show him which choices are right and which are wrong. He's sensitive to the difference between smiles and frowns, and he soon learns to understand "yes" and "no," as well as the caregiver's tone of voice and body language that indicate something is right or wrong. These outward cues guide the infant in making right choices, although he'll be about six years old before he will consistently be correct in discerning between right and wrong.

The Challenge

I sometimes ask people who attend my faith development seminar what an infant is like. What do infants enjoy? What do they do? Parents, grandparents and teachers who have infants raise their hands. "They like to hear singing." "They like to put

39

things in their mouths." "They like to watch faces." "They like to be held." These people are the experts on infants. They know what an infant likes.

If you spend time with one or more infants, you can do on a small scale what researchers do. Watch and listen. Find out what motivates the infant you work with. What does he like?

Now you have a challenge. You know what the infant does. You know what he likes. How can you communicate God to the infant through the things he does and likes? How can you make it **relevant** to his life? This is your challenge. But it's one you can meet. And you will be greatly rewarded for it.

Infancy

**Trust or Mistrust
(Hope)
Hebrews 11:1**

- seeds of faith
- creation
- care
- premoral stage
- sensorimotor stage
- egocentric

Chapter 5

Directors

Twos and Threes

"Does God have a paci (pacifier)?"
- 2 year old

The Task and the Strength

Early childhood, in this growth study, includes children two and three years old. I call them "directors," because they seem to want to direct everything. Someone once said, "Give me an army of two-year-olds, and I can take over the world."

Erikson says that the child at this stage develops either AUTONOMY or SHAME. An autonomous person is a person who rules himself. This is just what two and three year olds seem to want. They are beginning the process of becoming independent from Mom and Dad. They are becoming their own person.

Two- and three-year-olds want to do things for themselves. To help a child this age develop a sense of autonomy, adults can look for things the child can do. Show her what she can do: brush her teeth, wash her face, pick up toys, put on Velcro-fastened shoes, and many other things. As the child learns to be independent in these small ways, she feels a sense of AUTONOMY.

Of course, there are many things a young child is not able to do or is not allowed to do. The key to helping a child develop a sense of autonomy is the attitude of the adult. Encourage the child. If she needs help, step in to help her without criticizing and judging. Instead, express your confidence in her abilities. Show how proud you are that she's getting bigger and will one day be doing these things by herself.

If the child is not allowed to begin doing things for herself, or if she's constantly criticized and put down, she will develop a sense of shame. Erikson says shame is a feeling of being exposed. In this case, the child feels that what has been exposed is her own deficiency and inadequacy.

When the child moves through this stage feeling a sense of AUTONOMY, then the strength of WILL develops. Twos and threes are often called "strong willed" children. This is actually a good thing. God has planned for all of us to develop our own wills. He gives us free will. Then He asks us to choose to submit our wills to His. David wrote, "Teach me to do your will, for you are my God. . ." (Psalm 143:10).

Faith in Early Childhood

Fowler tells us that children are now forming their ideas and images of what God is like. They often think of God as having very human characteristics. Because of how Fowler describes this stage of faith development, I call it the "Fantasy/Imitative Stage." Fowler says this is "the fantasy-filled, imitative phase in which the child can be powerfully and permanently influenced by examples, moods, actions and stories" of the **significant adults** in her life. This stage of faith lasts until the child is about 6 or 7.

Imagination plays a big part in the lives of young children. As we learned earlier, they have difficulty distinguishing between fantasy and reality. So the made-up stories of TV superheroes and the real-life stories of Jesus' miracles may be given the same importance in the child's mind. It's good for us to point out what's real and what's not. But it's also important for us not to be surprised if young children still confuse the two.

Fowler emphasizes the adult's tremendous responsibility at this stage. He says, "The imagination and fantasy life of a child can be exploited by witting or unwitting adults." The religious stories, images and symbols we share with children "can prove life-opening and sustaining of love, faith and courage," or they can give rise "to fear, rigidity and the brutalization of souls." This is because young children generally believe what they are told, without questioning whether it is true or not. Young children are impressionable and trusting. They believe there's a Santa Claus because you tell them there's a Santa Claus. They believe there's a God and Jesus, because you tell them so. This is a stage of "taken-for-granted faith."

The "imitative" label on this stage is also important. Young children will imitate the **significant adults** around them. They cannot enter the adult's world, but they can imitate it. So the outward evidences of an adult's faith may be imitated by a young child. She may "play church," or pretend to pray, or baptize a stuffed animal.

The Significant Adult

Let's pause for a moment and look at the term **significant adult**. The question might be asked, "Who are the significant adults in the child's life?" The obvious, traditional answer is, "Mom and Dad." But this is not always the case. It's true that parents will always have a significant impact on their children, even if one or both parents are gone. The absence of a parent is indeed significant. However, I use the term **significant adult** to refer to an adult whose influence on the child affects the child's choices, the child's values.

The **significant adult** provides a moral compass for the child. In a radio interview, novelist Scott Spencer talked about the importance of a moral compass. "What do you do when you are physically away from your moorings?" he asked. It depends on your moral compass. The interviewer commented, "People close to us are our memory banks. They help explain our lives to us."[1] These are the people I'm referring to when I talk about the **significant adults** in a child's life.

To find out who the significant people are for a particular child *of any age*, ask, "Who spends time with the child? (Not just in the same house, but with the child.) Who listens to the child? Who plays with the child?" The answer to those questions will usually reveal the identity of the significant people in the child's life. And it may not always be adults.

What's Going on in the Young Child's Mind?

At this stage, most children use words in their communication, and they understand many more words than they use in their speech. If you listen to twos and threes, you can see that their perspective is still egocentric. They see the world only from their viewpoint, although that begins to change during the last half of this stage.

Piaget called this the "pre-operational" stage, which begins around age two and lasts until about age seven. "Operation" is a word Piaget used to describe a thought process that allows a child "to do in his mind what before was done physically." It describes logical reasoning. "Pre-operational" means that this stage of development comes before a child can reason logically. As we saw in Chapter 1, the young child operates by her own logic. One three-year-old exclaimed, "Mommy! I know why they call it the MOON!" Mom asked, "Why?" The little one answered, "Because the cow jumped over it and said MOOO!"

Twos and threes try to make sense of the world that revolves around their everyday activities, and they move through that world like a whirlwind, learning through their five senses. To find out how they affect the world, they perform simple cause and effect experiments: what will happen if I push this button, pull this string or take that apart? All this exploring keeps the adults around them hopping.

Developing Morality

As Erikson pointed out, **Will** is the strength that should develop at this stage. That's both good news and challenging news. Good news, because it means the child is growing and maturing. Challenging news, because it means the child is now aware that she can make deliberate choices. She struggles to learn the balance between exerting and submitting her will.

For toddlers this struggle is very difficult. They are just emerging from a completely egocentric stage. Everything they see, smell, taste, touch or hear is "mine." At about eighteen months, they begin to get a glimmer of understanding that other people have feelings and needs, too. Still, throughout this stage they continue to have a difficult time accepting the difference between "mine" and "yours." Their play reflects this possessiveness. They engage in what's called "parallel play": playing side by side, but not cooperatively together. However, a developmental milestone occurs as the child nears age three. She begins "perspective taking". This means she begins to be able to understand another's viewpoint and know that others have rights, opinions, possessions, and feelings just like hers.[2]

One mother told about her two-year-old daughter, who was not yet at the perspective-taking stage. The two-year-old hit another little girl. The mother was aghast, and asked her daughter, "How do you think that feels?" Her daughter responded by studying her fist and saying, "It felt pretty good." The two-year-old even interpreted the question egocentrically.

According to Dr. Lickona, this is a stage in which "right" is defined as "getting my own way." The reason to be good is so I will be rewarded and/or avoid punishment. So rules, consistently enforced, help train children to discern what's right and what's wrong. As we noted earlier, rules also help young children feel safe and secure. They sense their own difficulty in controlling themselves. So when there is a trustworthy person around to do the controlling, they don't have to be afraid of what might happen. They feel protected. One thing about toddlers: They usually have to be told the same rules over and over again. They have a hard time generalizing, understanding that a rule may apply everywhere, in all situations.

The Challenge

Do you know any two and three year olds? What do they like to do? What do they talk about? What do they like to play with? What do they like to see, hear, taste, smell and touch? What are they "into"? What games do they like to play? You can become the expert on twos and threes by watching and listening to them. Add your own observations to what you learned in this chapter.

Your challenge is to answer the question, "How do I communicate God to two- and three-year-olds using their interests? How can I make God's word relevant to the young child?"

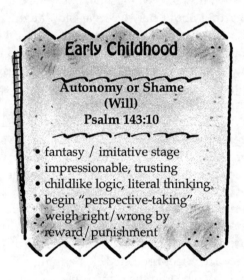

Early Childhood

**Autonomy or Shame
(Will)
Psalm 143:10**

- fantasy / imitative stage
- impressionable, trusting
- childlike logic, literal thinking
- begin "perspective-taking"
- weigh right/wrong by reward/punishment

Chapter 6

Discoverers
Fours and Fives

"Teacher! I'm five and nine quarters!
- 5 year old

The Task and the Strength

At this stage, children develop either INITIATIVE or GUILT. A person with initiative does things without being asked. He takes the offensive. He thinks independently. He's what we would call a self-starter. This describes children who are four and five years old. They are little scientists, trying to impose order on their rapidly expanding world, about which they have plenty of questions. They are out to explore, examine, and discover everything. They want to learn and know.

When a child is encouraged to follow this natural inclination to explore, he develops a sense of INITIATIVE. There are, of course, limits to what the four- or five-year-old child is able to do. There are also things he will not be allowed to explore. Again, it's the adult's response that is key to developing INITIATIVE. When the child is ridiculed or put down, or when he is continually restricted and told he is not capable, he begins to feel GUILT.

It's not that adults should let the child do anything he wants. But adults should have an encouraging attitude toward the child's God-given desire for knowledge and his attempts at exploration. There are encouraging ways to say, "No." For example, "I'm glad you want to dig in the dirt. But now is not the time. We'll plan another time when you can do that." Or, "This is not a good place to dig. Here's a better place." Sometimes, simply substituting an acceptable avenue of exploration for an unacceptable one solves the problem.

One area in which the curious child can easily swamp adults is with his questions. Young children ask hundreds of questions every day. Some of these questions are quite deep. When one of my sons was five, he asked, "Why does the skin on your body never end?" Other questions are so off-the-wall that they have no real, logical answers.

Frustrated adults sometimes respond with, "That's a silly question!" "Where did you come up with a question like that?" "I've had it with all these questions!" "I don't want to hear another question!" Responses like these cause the child to feel guilt. He doesn't know it's natural for him to ask questions. As far as he knows, he may be the only person in the world who is dumb enough not to know the answer.

There are some encouraging, initiative-promoting responses that are easy for adults to use. A good start is, "That's a good question!" It's always all right to say, "I don't know." It's even better to say, "What do you think?" Then the child can give his opinion. This helps him feel that his ideas and thoughts are valuable.

Sometimes the answer to a question is a matter of research, but the question comes at a time when it's not possible to look up the answer. Then a good response is, "We'll try to find out after lunch." Or "We'll try to find a book about that at the library." This not only values his question, but it helps him learn how to learn.

When a child develops his sense of INITIATIVE during this stage, the strength of PURPOSE emerges. The child feels, "There's a purpose for my curiosity. There's a purpose for my questions. There's a purpose for me in God's world." David felt the strength of purpose. He wrote, "The Lord will fulfill his purpose for me" (Psalm 138:8).

Faith in Four- and Five-Year Olds

Four- and five-year-olds are still in the Fantasy-Imitative stage of faith that began around age two. They are living what they imagine, and they are imitating the visible signs of faith of **significant adults**. One mother told about a baptism service at church. The children gathered around the baptismal pool and watched. Later that week, she took her five year old daughter and her cousins to the swimming pool where, she said, "They baptized each other all afternoon: You baptize me. I baptize you." For a more thorough review of this stage, see the Faith section in the previous chapter.

A young child's understandings are intuitive. He feels and understands without what we adults would classify as rational thought, although as the child grows, his ability to reason also grows. As we learned earlier, the young child believes whatever you tell him. That's why we often idealize the "pure" faith of a child. His faith is "taken-for-granted," and he does not question it. In other words, "that's just the way it is." And that's perfectly normal for this stage.

What's Going on in the Minds of Fours and Fives?

Fours and fives are still in what Piaget called the pre-operational stage, and they still learn primarily through their five senses. But significant mental skills are developing. Howard Gardner says that one of the most important skills that develops is the ability to understand and work with symbols. As the child grows from age two to around age six or seven, this ability increases. He grows from literal interpretations to understanding the symbolic.

Since there is so much symbolism and so many abstract concepts in Christianity, it's important to understand that preschoolers have very little capacity for understanding symbolism and thinking abstractly. This is an important factor not only in choosing Bible stories and concepts for preschoolers, but also in deciding how to teach. One mother told about going to a Christian bookstore with her five year old daughter. The little girl saw a painting of a lion lying down with a lamb. She pointed to the lamb and asked, "Is his name Worthy?"

Another mother was warning her preschool son to behave. She said, "You'd better stop that or you're going to be in hot water." Her son looked awed. "Mommy," he said, "why would you put me in hot water?" Fours and fives still interpret what we say literally.

Fours and fives also still use childlike logic. As one father and his young son walked down the front steps outside the front of the church building one Sunday, the little boy declared, "I know why we have cracks in our bottoms! It's so we can go down the stairs!" Another preschooler saw a house in a lot, sitting on the flat bed of a truck, which to an adult would indicate that the house was to be moved. But the child pointed to it and said, "That house must have been so dirty!" His mom asked, "Why?" The child said, "Because they had to lift it up to sweep all the dirt out from under it."

Fours and fives are beginning to realize that they are growing. They will not be babies forever. So they are very proud of their age. In fact, some of them may announce how old they are every time they come to class. This motivates other children to chime in and tell how old **they** are. This is a new concept to them: growing, getting older, better, smarter and stronger.

This interest in age may also have to do with the fact that children are now a great deal more interested in numbers and counting. In fact, Howard Gardner has called this an important "wave" in their growing ability to make and use symbols. Four-year-olds seem to want to count everything.

Because exploration and discovery are so much a part of their lives, fours and fives begin seeing a lot more of what's happening in the world around them. By five, they are also beginning to see the difference between fantasy and reality. But there's still a lot they don't understand, so they may develop fears they've not had before. They want and need understanding and comfort.

Developing Morality

Fours and fives still depend on rules (and the enforcement of those rules) to guide them in knowing and choosing what's right and what's wrong. However, their conscience is beginning to develop. The teaching and training of earlier years is beginning to be internalized. Now they don't have to be told as often. They know it's wrong to take toys from other children. It's right to share. It's wrong to hit. It's right to help. They are starting to understand the concept of consequences, cause and effect, if/then.

Dr. Robert Solomon, a professor of philosophy, points out that the conscience is, in many ways, the sensibility of "being caught in the act." In essence, we "catch ourselves." That's what moral education is. We learn to stop ourselves. "Our own self-consciousness imposes the internal judgment."[1]

Of course, children don't always go by what their developing conscience tells them (just as we don't always go by what our conscience tells us). They share selectively, picking and choosing what to share and when. They still have trouble seeing from any viewpoint but their own. They continue to need external help to confirm when they are on the right or wrong track. However, according to Dr. Lickona, around age five, children move up to a new level of morality, believing that what's right is to "do what I'm told."

We can see their new level of morality reflected in their play. Instead of "parallel play" (side by side but not together) of the twos and threes, we find fours and fives in "associative play." This means they start interacting cooperatively with other children when they play. You will hear things like, "You be the mommy and I'll be the baby." Or "You be the store man and I'll come and buy some food." Or "You make the road with the blocks and I'll drive my car over it."

Fours and fives also begin identifying with the values of the **significant people** in their lives. A five-year-old may report with dismay to Mom about a friend's family: "Do you know what movie *they're* going to watch tonight?" Or shocked, the five-year-old says, "Did you hear the word *he* said?" Four- and five-year-olds are discovering that not all people share the same values. As for them? They identify with your values, if you are one of the significant adults.

The Challenge

Do you know four- and five-year-old children? What are they "into?" What do they like and dislike? What do they enjoy doing, hearing, seeing, smelling, tasting? What games do they like to play? What do they talk about? Add your answers to the information you learned in this chapter. Your challenge is to decide how to communicate God to fours and fives through what they enjoy. Make it relevant to their lives. This is where you will be most successful.

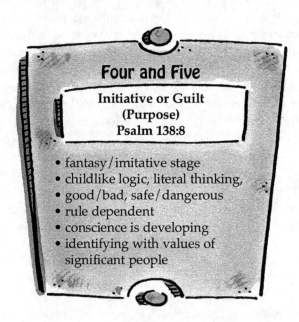

Four and Five

**Initiative or Guilt
(Purpose)
Psalm 138:8**

- fantasy/imitative stage
- childlike logic, literal thinking,
- good/bad, safe/dangerous
- rule dependent
- conscience is developing
- identifying with values of significant people

By now in the child's development, the most important character-shaping and faith-shaping years are almost over. Francis Xavier, a Jesuit leader, said, "Give me the children until they are seven, and anyone may have them afterwards."[2] The preschool years are perhaps the most important years of a person's life. Although major changes can and do happen later, by age six or seven, basic foundations have been laid within the child which will underlie the rest of his life. David Kherdian, in *The Road from Home*, wrote, "What you learn in old age is carved on ice. What you learn in childhood is carved on stone."[3]

Chapter 7

Collectors
Six through Nine

"Sometimes we say, 'I'm not playing with you
ever again!' But me and you say that all the time,
but come back in about an hour and say, 'Sorry.'
Besides, friends are friends, and friends we'll be forever."
- 8 year old

Who Are They?

The collector stage covers ages six through nine. Children this age collect things: rocks or baseball cards, stamps or stuffed animals, pennants or coins. Most of all, they collect friends. They want to be part of the group.

A great deal of development occurs during these years. There's a lot of difference between a six-year-old and a nine-year-old. Chip Wood, a principal and teacher, gives a good in-depth look at specific age differences and needs in his book *Yardsticks*. Briefly, here are some general characteristics he sees at each age:

SIX:
- sloppy, in a hurry
(Process is more important than product.)
- competitive, eager, enthusiastic

SEVEN:
- intense, conscientious, serious
- self-absorbed, self-conscious

EIGHT:
- speedy, energetic, full of ideas
- exploring their potential

NINE:
- worried, complaining, negative
- individualistic, prone to exaggeration[1]

The Task and the Strength

Erikson looked at this span of years and saw that children of these ages had something in common. He said these years were critical in creating either a sense of INDUSTRY or a sense of INFERIORITY.

An industrious person is someone who is busy doing productive things. That typifies six- through nine-year-olds. They want to use their developing physical skills. They want to see how fast they can run or how high they can jump. They want to make and build things. They want to be useful. When they are encouraged in their efforts to be busy and productive, they develop a sense of INDUSTRY.

INFERIORITY is the negative side of this stage and can develop in a variety of ways. If the adults in a child's life set goals that are too high, and the child cannot live up to their expectations, the child feels inferior. This is especially true if the child perceives that love and acceptance is conditional, based on her performance and achievement. For her, the consequences of failure are enormous.

If an adult does the child's work for her, the adult is planting seeds of inferiority. Adults know they can do projects faster and better. But when the adult takes over, the child gets the feeling that the adult thinks she is not capable. Her work is not good enough.

Inferiority can also develop if a child is not allowed to practice her skills. Every time she gets out the glue and paint, she is told, "Don't get all that stuff out again. You know all you'll do is make a big mess." It may not be the right time to "pull the stuff out," but the key to saying "no" is to say it in an encouraging way: "I'm so glad you're interested in building. Saturday afternoon you can build all you want."

This age child wants to know, "What do *I* do well?" Adults can play a key role by pointing out the child's strengths and accomplishments. "Jenny, I like the design in your painting. I believe you're an artist!" "You are so thoughtful, Bryan, to hold the door open for me!" And to Bryan later: "There's that thoughtful young man." Adults can give children a vision for who they are and what they can do.

When a child goes through this stage developing the positive sense of INDUSTRY, she reaps a bonus: the strength of COMPETENCE. She feels capable. This powerful asset is the basis for many accomplishments that lie ahead. Of course, as we point out children's skills, it's always appropriate to add, "I'm so glad God gave you that ability (or talent)." Because "Our competence comes from God" (2 Corinthians 3:5).

Faith in the Six- Through Nine-Year-Old

Competence breeds confidence. Confidence helps the child stand strong in her faith. It helps her share her faith with others. But what is her faith like at this stage? At the beginning of this stage, it is still primarily a taken-for-granted faith. Throughout this stage, children generally believe whatever you say. However, they usually begin asking insightful, and sometimes uncomfortable, questions. One six-year-old wanted to know, "Why is God a He, not a She?" A seven-year-old asked, "Why shouldn't the Palestinians shoot at Israel? Shouldn't the Palestinians get to fight back?"

A growing faith at this stage depends in large part on the stories the child sees and hears every day, especially the stories she sees and hears from the **significant adults** in her life. Because "story" plays such a big role, I call this is the "Story-Centered" stage of faith. According to Fowler, "the person begins to take on for him- or her- self the stories, beliefs and observances that symbolize belonging to his or her community."

What kind of stories affect the faith of children six through nine? The obvious stories are the Bible stories children read and hear. Children are particularly interested when we lead them to discover the historical and geographical settings of Bible stories, to examine real-life issues in the lives of biblical men and women and find out how God worked in their lives. Children at this age are ready to learn and understand that the Bible is not just a collection of stories, but is a whole story in itself.

But there are other kinds of stories that affect the faith of children who are six through nine. These are the random stories they hear from us. We tell stories all the time, although we may not realize it. Whenever we see a friend in the parking lot at the mall, we talk: "We just got back from vacation, and you'll never guess who I saw at church. I hadn't seen them in ages, and . . . and... and..." We are telling a story. The phone rings, and we visit with the person who called. We stand around and talk after church. We are telling our stories, and children are listening. They are intensely interested in knowing what it's like to be an adult.

To take advantage of this interest, we can begin telling children how God has worked and is working in our lives. We can invite other adults to tell their stories in our classrooms. These might be missionaries who are visiting, or someone who has come to God out of a life of drugs or atheism.

Then we can begin asking children to tell their stories. Fowler points out that this stage is a time when children have the ability to tell their own experiences. They can tell what God is doing in their lives. Together, their stories, your stories and Bible stories are strong faith builders.

During this time, children talk about church as if it were their club.[2] "My church does it this way. Jonathan's church does it that way. Here's what they do at Megan's church." It's not bad for a child to feel about church the way that he would feel about a club, because there's something very important that a club gives its members: a sense of belonging. We want the children who come to our churches to feel like they belong. They are valued members.

Children of this age begin to sense their need for God. They are seeing more of the world around them in schools, on teams, at piano lessons, at gymnastics. Their relationships now encompass other people from varied backgrounds, and they begin to experience the ups and downs of friendship and being in or out of favor with groups.

Younger children often believe that Mom and Dad can solve any problem. But now children begin to see that there are problems even Mom and Dad can't solve. Many children experience the difficulties of their parents' problems at home, some of which end in divorce or separation. All of this adds up to a strong sense of need for a faithful friend. Someone who is strong enough to protect. Someone who will stick around. Someone who is wise enough to solve any problem. They're sensing their need for God. Perhaps this is why many children accept Jesus as Lord during this time. They know they need Him.

What's Going on in the Mind of Six-through Nine-Year-Olds?

According to Piaget, the six-year-old is in her last year of moving from being pre-operational, unable to reason and think logically, to being "concrete operational." Piaget says the concrete operational stage lasts through age eleven. In this stage, the child is able to reason logically, but that applies only to something concrete, not abstract. In other words, the child has to see or handle something, it must be physically present or physically represented, for her to reason logically about it.

More recent research has shown that in some areas, children reach the concrete operational stage earlier. Howard Gardner says that a child may be pre-operational in the area of language, but concrete operational in the area of drawing or number.[3] This would account for some children who seem to understand symbolism, with concrete representations, in certain areas much earlier than age seven. However, age seven is often known as "the age of reason." By then most children have moved from literal interpretations of words, events, and stories to an understanding of symbolism and deeper meanings.

Children are now able to perceive distance and space more accurately. When children were younger, "long ago" meant yesterday. But now "long ago" means the distant past. They understand of the flow of time. So they begin to study events of history and can perceive them chronologically.

By age nine, children are in what some have called "the golden age of memory" because of their ability to retain a great deal of information. Many children seem to be able to memorize easily at this time.

Developing Morality

Between the ages of seven and nine, children develop the ability to tell whether something is true or false, right or wrong. But they still depend on rules to guide their behavior, and they are very alert to infractions of the rules. They are sensitive to justice and are quick to point a finger at those who have broken the rules. "It's not fair," is a common complaint. In fact, their focus is on fairness. They have an "eye for an eye, tooth for a tooth" sense of morality. However, they often have a double standard: Justice for all, mercy for me. Dr. Lickona tells us that they think "right" is to "look out for myself but be fair to those who are fair to me."

The Challenge

Do you know children who are in the age range of six through nine? What are they "into?" What do they like to do? What do they enjoy? What music do they like to listen to? What games do they like to play? What do they talk about? Add your answers to the information you learned in this chapter. Your challenge is to communicate God to them through what they are "into," through what they enjoy. How can you make God relevant to their world?

Elementary

**Industry or Inferiority
(Competence)
2 Corinthians 3:5**

- story-centered faith
- church is like a club
- sensing need
- literal to symbolic reasoning
- concrete operational
- loves projects
- rule oriented
- eye-for-eye morality

Chapter 8

Targets

Ten Through Twelve

"That story is SOOO boring!"
- 11 year old

Who Are They?

'Tweens (ages ten through twelve) are, of course, the in-betweeners, sandwiched in an awkward space between elementary-age children and the youth of adolescence. I call them targets, because advertising and the media focus a huge amount of attention on kids this age. They are indeed targets. Why? Because they are moving rapidly into a stage in which they are developing their identity, deciding who they are or at least how they would like to be perceived.

'Tweens are becoming body-conscious. It's all about image. And advertisers are hired to make consumers believe they must purchase and use certain products to enhance their image. They know parents spend more on 'tweens than on any other age group. "I'm a Pepsi guy." "I'm a (fill-in-the-blank with the popular brand) girl." Advertisers hope their products become part of the young person's identity.

I've called this an awkward stage, because 'tweens see-saw between being children and being youth. They have a foot in each world. Some 'tweens are most definitely still in the childhood stage. Others seem already to be very much like teenagers. Yet the bulk of them vacillate between child and teen, which is why you will see some of the previous stage reflected in the information below as well as previews of the coming adolescent stage.

As in the earlier stage, there's a great deal of difference between the younger and older ends of this group. Again, Chip Wood in *Yardsticks* gives a good look at each age specifically. In general, here are some characteristics:

TEN:
- relatively calm, cooperative, content
- quick to anger, but quick to forgive

ELEVEN:
- argumentative
- moody, sensitive, and self-absorbed

TWELVE:
- more reasonable and self-aware
- energetic and enthusiastic [1]

Perhaps the biggest leap is between ten and eleven. Parents usually experience the transition as a decrease in communication. The door to the 'tween's bedroom, which was always open before, is now closed and may have a sign on it: "Private." Or "Knock Before Entering." Or even "Keep Out." Boys become more restless. Girls become moody. Many girls begin menstruating, and moving into the world of emotional weather-patterns we might call "hormonal disturbances." This is another factor in making this an awkward stage, because boys usually enter puberty later than girls. Social groupings reveal this awkwardness. In previous stages, boys and girls generally mixed spontaneously during activities, but now they tend to gather in separate groups, and girls begin forming cliques.

The Task and the Strength

As in the previous stage, 'tweens have the task of continuing to develop a sense of INDUSTRY, but we can add the task of IDENTITY FORMATION. As we saw in the last chapter, developing a sense of industry involves the child discovering his skills and abilities. This discovery becomes a foundation for the 'tween's growing search for identity, which will continue through the teen years. This search for identity is obvious in the popularity of "My Space" and "Facebook," which allow for 'tweens and teens to craft an identity for themselves. It's also obvious in the brand-consciousness exploited by advertisers. "Brands are about giving you value, giving you self-esteem," says Juliet Schor in her book *Born to Buy*. [2]

The negative side of the equation is the sense of INFERIORITY discussed in the previous chapter. We can take that further now, adding the growing self-consciousness of the 'tween: How do I stack up in *their* eyes? What do they perceive about my image? The negative of IDENTITY FORMATION is IDENTITY CONFUSION, which will be discussed in more detail in the next chapter. For now, we can note that if a 'tween is developing a sense of industry and identity, the strength of COMPETENCE should begin emerging. FIDELITY (faithfulness) is the strength that grows out of identity formation, but we'll look at that in the next chapter, since adolescence is the time in which the process of identity formation reaches its peak.

Faith in 'Tweens

'Tweens are still sensing their need for God and still have the story-centered faith of the previous stage. They are greatly influenced by:

- the stories of their faith community
  (Who are we as a church? Do we send out lots of missionaries? Do we take part in evangelistic crusades? Do we focus on helping single-parent homes? Do we build houses with Habitat for Humanity?)
- the stories told in word and deed by the **significant adults** in their lives
  (Why are my parents and extended family Christians, or why are they not? Do they do what they teach? What are their values as shown by the story of their lives? Whose stories do they listen to?)

- their own stories as they share them with each other
    (Do the adults in my life care to hear what I have to
    say? Are they interested in the stories of my life?
    Will they respond over-the-top emotionally, or will
    they listen?)

Juliet Schor points out another type of story that all stages have to deal with, but one that seems all-pervasive in this Target stage. That's the stories told by our consumer culture. She says corporations have become "our children's 'story-tellers' and the dominant transmitters of culture" through the media and advertising. [3]

Another cultural factor is pluralism. A pluralistic society is one in which each different ethnic, racial, religious, and social group keeps its own identity and culture within a common civilization. [4] That describes our society today. 'Tweens now measure their beliefs against the beliefs of others. They may wonder how their Buddhist or Hindu or Muslim friend at school can be such a good person when that friend doesn't believe in Jesus. They may express amazement that their friends of different religions are just as committed and passionate about their beliefs as Christians at church are about their own faith. In addition, 'tweens see our inconsistencies, have lots of important questions, and may begin challenging, perhaps even arguing with, the beliefs they have been taught and have, until now, taken for granted. This may make us feel uncomfortable, but it is completely normal at this stage in the faith development process, and it leads logically into the next stage of faith, as we will see.

What's Going On In the Minds of 'Tweens

The 'tween stage is the second fastest time of brain growth and capacity (infancy to age five is the fastest). [5] This marks the transition into the stage that Piaget calls "formal operational," which starts around the age of twelve. With formal operations, teens begin to be able to reason logically and more like adults. We'll talk more about this in the next chapter. One of the welcome benefits of this brain growth is that 'tweens can concentrate longer than children in earlier stages can.

Another factor of brain growth has to do with being able to process reality maturely. The good news is that this brain growth is a signal that maturity is coming. The bad news is that it doesn't happen overnight. It develops over time. A fairly long time. Psychologist Daniel Golman says, "The prefrontal-limbic neural circuitry crucial to the acquisition of social and emotional abilities is the last part of the human brain to become anatomically mature, a developmental task not completed until the mid-twenties."[6]

When we looked at the stage of early childhood, we noted that children are not able consistently to tell the difference between fantasy and reality until they are about five years old. But there is a type of fantasy that continues through the 'tween and even teen years. We might call it "wishful thinking." It goes something like this: "Me? I can drink beer and not get drunk." "I won't get pregnant." "I can drive without a license and not get caught." "I won't get an STD." Those things may happen to other people, but not to ME. For girls, this type of fantasy lasts until around the ages of sixteen or seventeen. For boys, it lasts into their early twenties. So here, again, when we discuss 'tweens, we find ourselves flowing right into the next stage.

Developing Morality

Where are 'tweens morally? Again, we can look at both the previous stage as well as the stage to come. 'Tweens still have the rule-oriented, fairness-focused, double-standard morality that characterizes younger kids. But they are beginning to challenge boundaries that seem arbitrary to them.

Because of their maturing mental capacities, 'tweens can be good at thinking through social issues and suggesting solutions. They can also do a better job of gauging right and wrong, but they may act or speak impulsively without thinking about the consequences. They tend to test the limits as they grow through this stage and begin thinking more about teen dilemmas. The biggest influences on their values are television, peers, school, parents, internet, and magazines [7], and they tend to conform to the wishes of the **significant people** in their lives, the people who spend time with them, work and play with them, and really listen to them when they have something to say.

Defying Definition

Before we end our look at 'tweens, let's hear from two teachers who love this sandwiched, targeted group. The first is Jennifer Weinblatt, who says kids at this stage defy definition.

". . . Every year in my classroom there are small, skinny boys with big ears and knobby knees who like board games and computers. Sitting beside them are boys whose growth spurts have already begun, who hang out in skate boarding parks and idolize Jimi Hendrix.

"And the girls . . . the girls are everywhere: quiet, flat chested and bespectacled; bosom-sprouting and brassiered; mall crazy and sports crazy and boy crazy and boy fearful. They are dressed in tight jeans and cropped tops or warm-ups and baggy T-shirts, toting *YM Magazine* and lip gloss or Hello Kitty purses and stuffed bunnies.

"Sixth grade is characterized by contradiction; that is what I love about it."[6]

The second is Ann Parr, a good friend of mine, who teaches writing to kids. Ann describes the 'tweens she works with as open and able to ask for what they need. "Don't believe all the media tells you about these kids," she says. "They're communicators, resilient and expressive. If they don't like it, they'll say so, or walk out if they can. But they give me hope. They are so fun and funny. Many of them have lived through divorce and abuse, and they've come out without much fear." In the 'tweens Ann works with, she's seen politeness, genuine expressions of gratitude, and concern for others.

The Challenge

Do you know kids who are in the age range of ten through twelve? What are they "into?" What do they like to do? What do they enjoy? What music do they like to listen to? What games do they like to play? What do they talk about? Add your answers to the information you learned in this chapter. Your challenge is to communicate God to them through what they are "into," through what they enjoy. How can you make God and His word relevant to their world?

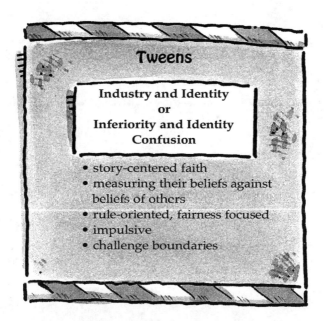

Tweens

**Industry and Identity
or
Inferiority and Identity
Confusion**

- story-centered faith
- measuring their beliefs against beliefs of others
- rule-oriented, fairness focused
- impulsive
- challenge boundaries

Chapter 9

Becomers

Adolescents

---

*A parent commented to his 14-year-old
that math these days was much easier,
because kids can use a calculator to solve the problems.
His son responded, "Easier? No way. Math is hard.
You have to learn which buttons to push."*

Who Are They?

For this study, adolescence describes ages thirteen through nineteen. However, since this book focuses on communicating with the child living at home and attending our children's and youth classes, we'll stop with age seventeen, the age at which most youth graduate from our high school programs.

I recently taught a series on the life of Jesus in historical context to the youth of our church, who ranged in age from twelve through seventeen. Every Sunday after my large-group lesson, they split into eight smaller groups for discussion: seventh and eighth grade girls, seventh and eighth grade boys, ninth and tenth grade girls, ninth and tenth grade boys, eleventh and twelfth grade girls, eleventh and twelfth grade boys. Each group had at least one adult, and usually two, to help guide the conversation. Our youth leaders are still discussing the best way to divide the age groups, but they know that it's awkward to have twelve-year-olds and seventeen-year-olds in the same group. There is a great difference between the youngest and the oldest in this age range. To most effectively communicate with the give-and-take of discussions and activities, they need to be in groups with kids close to their own age. Here's a general breakdown of traits to be aware of:

THIRTEEN:
- boys lag behind girls about a year in signs of physical maturity
- peer pressure increases
- can be touchy, withdrawn, sarcastic, worried about school work

FOURTEEN:
- boys now entering puberty
- identity tends to be wrapped up in the peer group
- distancing from adults

FIFTEEN:
- desire to be accepted
- establishing their own value system
- want to do it their way
- may argue for argument's sake[1]

SIXTEEN:
- idealistic; may be disillusioned
- more individual, less group-focused
- strong convictions, strongly expressed

SEVENTEEN:
- embodies both a sophisticated adult and a sensitive youth
- both sexes are physically mature and interested in each other[2]

The Task and the Strength

Kids in this age bracket are not children anymore. They are young men and women, young adults. They are beginning the last stage of what began in infancy: becoming an independent individual. It's no surprise then that their main task is to develop a sense of IDENTITY. As you remember, this task began in the previous stage. It now intensifies as the adolescent tries to figure out who he is, what he believes, and where he plans to go. He explores different roles that are available to him, and he chooses a path to pursue for the future.

For this reason, adolescents continue to be targets for the marketing pitches of almost anyone and everyone who has a product to sell. They are "a market segment worth an estimated $150 billion a year."[3] In an in-depth look at marketing and the youth culture, commentator David Kupelian stated that "teenagers increasingly look to the media to provide them with a ready-made identity predicated on today's version of what's cool."[4] But, he points out, advertising and media are interested in promoting a consumer identity, not necessarily a healthy identity.

Money is the marketers' ultimate goal, but health is ours. One way parents and teachers can encourage teens to develop a healthy sense of identity is to listen to them and let them question. Teens often try ideas on for size. Sometimes they express themselves very strongly in certain areas just to hear themselves take a stand – often a stand that they know is different from that of the adult they're talking to. They are trying to say what the two-year-old discovered so long ago: I am a person in my own right. I am not you.

Anastasia Goodstein, publisher of Ypulse, an online news and commentary site about Generation Y, gives us a good description of the identity-seeking teen through the popularity of "MySpace" and other similar sites. She says, "'Teens are narcissistic and exhibitionist. For teens, especially, who are going through this stage where they're constantly looking for that affirmation and validation and response for everything they are, it's addictive."[5]

Allowing teens to make more and more of their own decisions as they move through the teen years helps them navigate the waters toward establishing their own identity. They need to wobble around where it's safe and they still have adult support. If the teen is still treated like he's a ten-year-old, if his views and opinions are not valued and listened to, or if someone maps out his future paths for him, he will develop a sense of IDENTITY CONFUSION. But teens do need loving adult support and appropriate youth-sensitive boundaries.

Raising a teen is a bit like flying a kite. You toss the kite into the air, holding tightly to the string. Little by little, you let the string out, watching it bob around on the air currents. At times, you reel it in a little; at times, you lengthen the tether. In parenting, you eventually take the scissors out of your pocket and cut the kite string so it can take off and soar on its own.

If a teen is developing his own sense of identity, the strength of FAITHFULNESS becomes his. Faithfulness, one of the fruits of the Spirit (Galatians 5:22, 23), means being faithful, or dedicated, to your beliefs and values. It means being true to who you are, or in the case of faith development, to whose you are.

Faith in Adolescence

Because the adolescent is trying to establish identity, the teen years are a time to personalize faith. Teens are involved in and affected by many arenas of life, including family, school, peers, work, the media, church groups, hobbies, and other interests. Fowler says a teen needs to understand how faith relates to all these involvements in order to make his faith personal and real. Faith "must provide a basis for identity and outlook," and faith must operate not only in the area of inspiration, but also in the realm of practical interaction with today's world.

Ultimately, no arena in which the young person is involved will fulfill him in and of itself. Disappointments and difficulties are common as adolescents begin to realize this truth. Kevin Huggins, a professor of counseling, talks about this in his book *Parenting Adolescents.* He writes, "One of the most important developmental tasks an adolescent has to accomplish (is) to come to the realization that his deepest desires cannot be met anywhere except in a relationship with Christ."[6] The teen needs to find in God someone who loves and accepts him and has actually placed within him the deepest desires of his heart.

During this stage, questions and tension abound. Teens may rebel against take-for-granted beliefs, not in the sense of revolting, but in the sense of refusing to "buy in." However, this is part of what leads the teen toward achieving a personal faith. He does not want to simply imitate his parents' faith or his friend's faith, or his youth group's faith. He wants to develop a strong relationship with Jesus on his own so that he can know that these are *his* beliefs, *his* values, *his* faith.

After all is said and done, a Christian's identity is found in who he is in Jesus. Christ in us. Jesus becomes the source and essence of our identity as we grow up in faith. This is where we hope our teens are headed, and the path we want to help them find.

What's Going on in the Adolescent's Mind?

By now, the adolescent has entered into the formal operational stage, according to Piaget. He is maturing, beginning to reason logically, becoming able to think about abstract concepts and hypothetical situations and think about thinking. He begins to see many options open to him, which may make decision-making difficult. But as this stage progresses, his thinking becomes more like an adult.

However, Kevin Huggins reports that many teens choose not to use formal thinking. Why? Maybe because of stress. Maybe because formal thinking often grows through pain and problems, and these are things we try to avoid. Maybe because the best way to develop mature thinking is to interact with other people who are thinking maturely.[7] Many young people spend most of their time associating with their peers and very little time associating with mature adults.

Another characteristic of teens is their tendency to exaggerate. They often have "over-the-top" reactions. And they often contradict themselves. A sixteen-year-old girl proclaims, "I can't stand chocolate." Later, she says, "Snickers! That's my favorite candy!"

Developing Morality

Novelist Orson Scott Card writes that the life of the adolescent is "full of passion, intensity, magic, and infinite possibility; but lacking responsibility, rarely expecting to have to stay and bear the consequences of error. Everything is played at twice the speed and twice the volume in the adolescent – the romantic – life."[8] That's a reminder of the "wishful thinking" type of fantasy again, the "it won't happen to me" mindset. As I mentioned earlier, this type of fantasy lasts until around sixteen or seventeen for girls, into the early twenties for boys.

An adolescent is very conscious of other people's opinions, particularly their opinions about him, because his mind can now reason formally. He can think about what others might be thinking about him. He may also contemplate how different value systems would work in his life. He's looking for what "fits" him. He may doubt his parents' viewpoint, yet turn around and swallow the tales of the world around him, hook, line, and sinker.

As a writer for young adults, I find coming-of-age novels fascinating. They show the adolescent's search for identity, which of course reflects the real-life struggles of real-life teens, but usually in a time-limited frame. Kelly Bingham, a YA writer and mother of teens, has compiled a list of some of these changes. She says that a teen protagonist often enters his or her story with one or more of the following: self-doubt, bitterness, anger, self-centeredness, jealousy, depression, guilt, refusing to mature, blaming others for their problems, wondering where they fit in, and/or wondering "who am I?" The adversity the teen faces in the novel at first creates a surge of self-doubt and no obvious way forward, says Bingham. By the end of the story, the teen has worked through his or her problems. Although they still have more maturing to do, teen protagonists have at least learned one or more positive traits: resourcefulness, bravery/courage, empathy/concern for others, the ability to ask for help, gratitude, resilience, hope, a conscious choice to mature, self-awareness, and a conscious search for who they are and where they belong. Bingham says these positive traits are what they can cling to when things get tough.[9]

But how do these changes come about? Through conflict, hardship, pain, and problems. As teens face challenges head-on, we adults need to allow them to feel the challenge, grapple with it, and grow through it, instead of trying to help them avoid or eliminate their pain. Orson Scott Card says, "Only when the loneliness becomes unbearable do adolescents root themselves, or try to root themselves. It may or may not be in the community of their childhood, and it may or may not be their childhood identity and connections that they resume upon entering adulthood."[10] Of course, we pray that the teen finds his ultimate hope in God and His gift of love and grace in Jesus.

Since one of the teen's strong desires is to be accepted, his morality tends to be a "conformist morality." When he has a decision to make between right and wrong, he will ask, "What will **they** think of me if I do this (or if I don't do this)?" The they in question are the people who are **significant** to him. **They** might be his school peer group, or his church youth group, or his youth director or teacher, or his parents. But the **significant** people in his life will become part of his moral compass.

Chip Wood points out that community service helps build moral strength. To this end, we need to involve young people in missions, serving the poor, disaster relief, building houses for needy families, emergency first-aid, and other areas of service. We can also train teens in the practical, real-life skill of mediation, helping others make peace. Serving others helps kids feel needed. It gives them something significant to accomplish and prepares them for the future. It can become part of the teen's growing sense of identity. In fact, there is a growing group of teens who are expressing a "deep-seated exasperation" over the fact that they are "essentially deprived of opportunity to do their best – through 'low expectations' of society."[11] They resent being thought of as the church of tomorrow. They are the church of today.

It's interesting to note that a strong identity helps people resist temptation. Only when a young person knows who he is and what he believes can he be faithful to his beliefs and values. Isaiah told King Ahaz, "If you do not stand firm in your faith, you will not stand at all" (Isaiah 7:9). Standing firm is faithfulness.

The Challenge

Do you know any teenagers? What do they like? What are they "into?" What do they enjoy doing? What kind of music do they like? What kinds of games do they play? What do they talk about? You'll notice a variety of personalities, and a variety of likes and dislikes. Is there common ground?

Look at your answers to these questions. Add that to the information you learned in this chapter. Now your challenge is to communicate God and His Word to teens through what they enjoy. How can you communicate in ways they can understand? How can you make God relevant to their world?

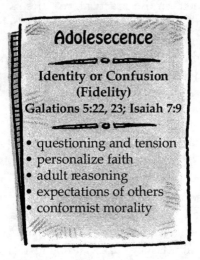

Adolesecence

**Identity or Confusion
(Fidelity)
Galations 5:22, 23; Isaiah 7:9**

- questioning and tension
- personalize faith
- adult reasoning
- expectations of others
- conformist morality

Chapter 10

What If?
Two Questions About Stages

*Eighty to ninety percent of Christian young people
leave the church after graduation from high school.*
- Dr. Brad Widstrom[1]

Finding Faith – or Losing It?

At this point, it would be unfair of us to leave the issue of faith development without addressing the current phenomenon that has sent many teachers, parents, and youth leaders scrambling for answers: The majority of youth leave the church after graduating from high school. Statistics vary according to who you listen to, but the numbers are well over 75%. I've dealt in depth with this in another book, so I won't repeat myself here. But I do want to point out the thread we have followed as we've gone through the developmental stages.

- Preschoolers   take beliefs for granted
- Six – eight   generally believe, but may ask astute questions
- Nine – ten   ask questions, see inconsistencies
- Eleven   may challenge beliefs
- Twelve   may argue with beliefs
- Thirteen and up   may rebel against beliefs, not in the sense of revolting, but in the sense of refusing to "buy in"

You may say that your child or even most of the kids in your 'tween or youth group are not challenging, arguing, or rebelling. That doesn't mean they don't have questions or concerns. It may mean they are afraid to express those concerns. Or it may mean it hasn't occurred to them yet to truly personalize their faith. Or they may equate mental assent to their parents' beliefs with a personal faith. But in order for a teen to personalize faith, he or she must drop the taken-for-grantedness of it.

In this regard, I see three options for the adolescent:

1. Don't question the taken-for-grantedness.

   In this case, the answer to "Why do you believe?" is "Because my mom and dad (or pastor or youth leader) told me it was so."

2. Let go of taken-for-granted belief and pick up personal faith.

   In this case, the expression of your young person's faith may or may not look like yours. But it will be her own personal faith, and she will be able to explain from her heart-felt conviction why *she* is a Christian, and not just say by rote what she has been taught to say.

3. Drop the taken-for-grantedness of faith and leave it behind.

   This seems to be what a lot of young people are doing. At least they are leaving the church behind. (Which might put them in a new category: having a personal faith in Jesus that is expressed outside the traditional church.)

The question is: Why would kids not personalize the Christian faith as part of their developing identity? Or why would they personalize faith yet leave the church, if indeed that's what some of them are doing? That, of course, is a broad subject and one I cover in another book. If you are interested in exploring these issues, I invite you to join me in the book *I Want to Believe But I Can't*.

What If the Scale was Tipped to the Negative?

Another question about stages: What if a person didn't develop the positive? What if she didn't gain a sense of trust in infancy? What if she didn't develop a sense of industry and competence in her school years? Does she get stuck at that stage?

The answer is no. A person progresses through all the stages. We can compare it again to building a house. All the floors will be added on, one by one. If the negative side of a stage develops instead of the positive side, the person will move on, carrying with her the negative sense that she received from that stage. As an adult, she may have an underlying sense of shame or undue guilt. She may feel inferior. Or she may not have a strong sense of identity. There's a crack in the foundation that may cause problems in the house later on.

What can we do if someone has developed the negative instead of the positive? Here are some things to remember:

1. Children are very resilient. They bounce back and usually forgive easily. Just because there's a crack somewhere doesn't mean the house will fall down. Everyone has "issues," and the way we respond to them can make us stronger and wiser.

2. God is in control. None of us is perfect. At one time or other, we all add weight to the negative side of the child's development. As we work with children at home or in the classroom, we need to pray, "Father, make up for my deficiencies as a parent or teacher." In Joel 2:25, God promises his people, "I will repay you for the years the locusts have eaten." God can patch the cracks, though He may not do so miraculously, and there may be some healing pain involved.

3. You can help repair the damage. If the damage is causing serious problems, the person should see a Christian counselor to help her work through the pain of the past so that it no longer has a stranglehold on her present or future. However, let's say you know or suspect that a child you are working with has experienced abandonment and never developed a sense of trust. In that case, you show her that you are trustworthy and your love

and respect for her are unconditional. She will probably test you to see if that's true. So you stay the course. Show you're trustworthy by loving her no matter what.

Whether a person missed out on trust or autonomy or initiative or industry or identity, your role is the same. Accept and encourage by giving the person doses of the positive input that she missed at that earlier stage in life.

Stages of FAITH*

An Overview

Teens
Identity or
Identity Confusion
(Faithfulness)

Tweens
Industry & Identity
or
Inferiority & Identity
Confusion

Elementary
Industry or
Inferiority
(Competence)

Four and Five
Initiative or Guilt
(Purpose)

Early Childhood
Autonomy or Shame
(Will)

Infancy
Trust or Mistrust
(Hope)

* following Erik Erikson's
tasks and strengths

Communication
IN THE
CLASSROOM

Chapter 11

From the Heart the Mouth Speaks

Communicating with Children

Child: "Why *don't* we pray for the West Coast?"
Mom: "We do, sweetheart. We pray for the whole world."
Child: "But at church, we say, 'In the name of the Father,
the Son and the whole East Coast.'"

Peter Smith, a specialist in children's literature and learning skills, tells about the time he took his preschool daughter to a dairy farm. She watched intently as the cows were milked by the milking machines. Mr. Smith was very pleased that his daughter would have a head start when she got to school, having learned about the farm.

But a few weeks later, Mr. Smith found that his daughter hadn't quite understood. As he reminisced about the dairy farm with his daughter, she commented, "Those cows sure drink a lot of milk." She had thought the milk was going into the cows instead of coming out.

As an exercise in communication, read the dialogue in the following boxes. If you have trouble, read it aloud slowly.

M R DUCKS.
M R KNOT.
O S A R.
C M WANGS?
L I B, M R DUCKS.

M R SNAKES.
M R KNOT.
O S A R.
C M B D I'S?
L I B, M R SNAKES.

M R FARMERS.
M R KNOT.
O S A R.
C M M T POCKETS?
L I B, M R FARMERS.

M R MICE.
M R KNOT.
O S A R.
C M E D B D FEET?
L I B, M R MICE.

Did U C? Sometimes children find our communications with them as confusing as the above exercise may have appeared at first glance. Let's see what we can do to make sure we communicate as clearly as possible.

Non-Verbal Communication

Misunderstandings happen, even among adults, of course. While clarity in communication can be critically important, it's usually no big deal. But since we're in the business of communicating, let's look at ways we can increase our chances of being understood.

First of all, we should realize that most of our communication is done without words. We communicate through our tone of voice. Try saying, "I love you" in a sarcastic tone of voice. What will that communicate to the listener? People believe our tone of voice more than the words we speak.

Another factor in communication is body language. Tightly folded arms indicate a protective, impatient, or defensive attitude. Droopy shoulders spell discouragement. For communicating with a child, good body language includes getting on the child's level so you can literally "see eye to eye." A gentle, friendly pat on the arm or shoulder can also help.

Then there are facial expressions. A smile can indicate welcome and warmth. Tightly closed lips and clenched teeth give away anger.

A UCLA researcher, Albert Mehrabian, did a study to see just how important these non-verbal cues are in our communication. He found that 50% of our communication comes from what people see when we talk to them: our body language, gestures, and even our appearance. Our tone of voice communicates 38% of what they hear. Only 7% of what we communicate comes through our actual words, the content of what we say.[1]

Stop, Look and Listen

Our study of developmental stages positions us to communicate well, because one of the important factors in communication is being aware of "where" children are mentally, morally and spiritually. In a way, we are like missionaries going into another culture. We have to learn to speak the language. We have to try see the world through children's eyes. We must also listen.

For several years, I taught writing classes for upper elementary grades, junior high and high school. One assignment required fifth graders to write a paper entitled "What Am I?" Some of the papers were very revealing. One girl wrote:

> What am I? A best friend to some, an enemy to others, a little voice coming from behind the wall that no one hears.

Another girl wrote:

> What am I? I am the little girl in the ballerina suit twirling and spinning around and around. The little girl who got up on stage and sang a song at preschool graduation. The little girl with food on her face. I am the little girl walking just in a diaper. I am also the little schoolgirl doing her homework. I am just a painting on the wall that nobody hardly looks at.

Children know when no one is listening. Their feelings are no different than ours: When somebody listens to us, we feel valued.

But it's not only children who benefit when an adult listens to them. The adult benefits as well. We gain insights into the child's needs and interests. Remember the questions asked at the end of most of the previous chapters. "Do you know a child this age? What do they like?" and so on. The better you know a child, the better positioned you are for communicating with him.

I taught four-year-olds at church for many years. At the beginning of one year, we had in our class a little boy who was particularly rambunctious. Jonathan couldn't seem to keep his hands off the other children. It was hard for him to focus on the learning activities. Since I was the supervising teacher, when the children went to different activities, I roved from center to center, making sure everything was all right. I would watch and listen and help wherever I was needed.

One day, I happened to be visiting Jonathan's group. They were drawing pictures. I thought I heard Jonathan say he was drawing a cougar. I knelt beside him and watched. His lips were pressed tight. His eyes glared at the paper. He was mashing down hard with his crayon, drawing big, dark circles, around and around and around.

I said, "Jonathan, I like the colors you're using to make your cougar."

"It's not a cougar," said Jonathan. He kept making circles, gazing at his paper. "It's a big, fat female."

I was so surprised, I wanted to laugh. But I didn't. (One rule of communication: Don't laugh at what kids say unless they are trying to tell a joke. Usually when a preschooler says something funny, it's serious. Their "jokes" are usually not funny.)

Anyway, I didn't say anything, not because I thought this was an important listening moment, but because I couldn't think of anything to say. I just kept watching and listening. Then Jonathan said something that opened a big door of understanding.

Drawing circles furiously, and without looking up at me, he said, "My mommy and my daddy is makin' problems, and my daddy is gonna' move out."

All of a sudden, I knew why Jonathan behaved the way he did in class. He was angry and confused and lost. He didn't know how to handle his feelings.

Jonathan taught me that listening is extremely important. It helps us know where kids are mentally, morally, spiritually and emotionally. Robert Coles, author of *The Spiritual Life of Children*, was asked in an interview, "Do you think we miss out on opportunities to know children by failing to listen to them?"

He answered, "Yes, I do. Remember, Jesus said that the children in some way will be a clue to eternity. Children were not meant to be put in the straitjackets that some of us want them to be in, to hold their breath until they grow up. They offer us a chance to see a good part of what we are: human beings struggling to figure out what this world means. They ask all sorts of wonderful questions in that regard."[2]

How can we learn to communicate better? We can stop, look and listen.

Play

Dr. Robert Hemfelt, a psychologist, and Dr. Paul Warren, a behavioral pediatrician, have co-authored several books about parent-child relationships. They say that "play is the single most effective way to communicate with children less than nine years old."[3] Why? Play provides a comfortable format for communication.

I once heard a radio interview with a woman named Kelly Bates who worked at Vanderbilt Hospital in Nashville, Tennessee. Her job was to help children who came to the hospital to undergo a traumatic type of treatment or who had already been through a trauma. She was once asked, "How do you get children to trust you? They don't know you, and you are only with them for a short time." She answered simply, "I play with them."

When you play with children, you get to know each other. You build relationship. Children grow to trust you, because you are showing you value them. You are communicating that they are important enough for you to give them one of your most precious possessions: time.

This is true not only for young children, but also for 'tweens and teens. My husband and I experienced this in our own family. When our sons were teenagers, some of our best conversations occurred as we played together. Sometimes we played cards. Sometimes we played badminton. Sometimes we played catch or shot baskets. Working together can serve the same function. When you are focused on something other than the child, barriers come down and conversation is freer.

One mother told me she had experienced this with one of her three sons. They were teenagers, and their grandmother had died. One son in particular had not been able to mourn, and he seemed closed for discussion about the death. Their family had the habit of playing cards together. During one of their card games, this son paused and said, "I miss Grandmother." Play relaxed the barriers and opened the door for communication.

> Play relaxed the barriers and opened the door for communication.

How does this translate to the classroom? We teachers should not only direct activities, but also join and enjoy them. We should not be afraid to play and work with children, because it provides a great format for communication.

Give Positive Instructions

Children often hear, "Don't do this. Don't do that." Life is full of "don'ts." But telling children what to do is often more effective than telling them what not to do. It may take some practice, but we can learn to express most of our instructions in a positive way.

I was once demonstrating teaching techniques to a group of parents. As I handed paper cups to the children, I said, "Keep the cups in a cup shape." The parents laughed at me, and I admit, my instructions did sound funny. I could have said, "Don't crush the cups." Instead, I deliberately tried to be positive. Sometimes this results in creative sentences!

But there are definite advantages to being positive, besides just encouraging positive thinking. First of all, if I had said, "Don't crush the cups," I would have given that idea to several children who hadn't thought of it yet. Second, by being positive, I limited their alternatives.

For example, if I want my class to walk down the hall quietly, it would be a mistake to say, "Don't run." Why? Because that would leave many other options. Kids could skip, roll, dance, jump and find lots of other creative ways to get down the hall. They would still be obeying me, as long as they were not running. But if I say, "Walk quietly," I give them only one option, my choice.

In one of the Laura Ingalls Wilder books, Laura and her sister Mary spend a day sliding down the straw-stack. When Pa comes home, he is upset, because the straw is now scattered across the yard, and he has to re-stack it. He says, "You girls mustn't slide down the straw-stack any more."

After dinner, Laura and Mary take a walk outside. They amble close to the straw-stack and begin sniffing it. Soon Laura is rolling in the straw. "Come on, Mary!" she calls. "Pa didn't say we can't roll!"

Pa is angry until he sees how the girls have interpreted his instructions. He ends up by saying that the straw "MUST - STAY - STACKED." He learned to state his instructions in a positive way instead of negative.[4]

Choose Words Carefully, Speak them Clearly

Sometimes children misunderstand us because they don't know the meaning of the words we use. So they assume we are saying a similar word that they do know.

One little girl heard that a mean teacher at her school had been fired. She went home and told her parents that the supervisor had burned up the mean old teacher.

One family passed a smelly meat-packing plant every Sunday on their way to church. The mother told the kids that the bad smell came "from the plant over there." A few years later, on a vacation, they smelled the same bad smell. One of the children pointed to a tall weed and said, "It must come from the plant over there."

Other times, children misunderstand because we don't enunciate our words clearly, or we speak too quickly or too softly. A friend of mine grew up in a church where they often sang the song, "Lead On, O King Eternal." He always thought they were saying, "Lead On, O Kinky Turtle."

One five year old boy came home from Sunday school asking, "What's a weeklebutt?" The child became more and more frustrated when his dad could not tell him. Finally more information came out. "You know," the child said. "We are weeklebutt. He is strong." Dad had to explain the words to the familiar song "Jesus Loves Me."

Misunderstandings not only happen with young children, but with teens and adults as well. I once heard a pastor say in his sermon, "We all have fallen genes." But the word "genes" was heard as "jeans." A muffled laughter spread across the congregation. It took a moment before the pastor realized what he had said.

Some misunderstandings are inevitable. But we can minimize them by choosing our words carefully and speaking them clearly.

Use Good Manners

Speak to children respectfully. Remember "please" and "thank you." Even when you must be firm, be courteous. Never call children names or belittle them. Our attitude toward children should not be one of condescension, but of respect.

Remember when Jesus' disciples argued over who was the greatest? Jesus took a little child and brought him into their group. He said, "Whoever welcomes this little child in my name welcomes me; and whoever welcomes me welcomes the one who sent me. For he who is least among you all – he is the greatest" (Luke 9:48).

Pay attention to the way you welcome children into your room. Treat the child the way you would treat an adult. Greet him by name. Smile at him. Listen to him. Talk to little children in a normal tone of voice and not with "baby talk."

Be careful about teasing children, especially young ones. Teasing can confuse a child about what you really mean, and sometimes it is received as mockery and criticism. Teasing can easily make a child feel stupid. We want children to feel loved and valued.

Taking the time and effort to communicate effectively with children will reap great rewards for teachers. After all, we are to reflect Jesus to those around us, including children. Henrietta Meers said, "First I learned to love my teacher. Then I learned to love my teacher's God."[5] That is the goal.

Chapter 12

Wired For Learning
Individual Learning Differences

"Where did the thunder go? In back of the world?"
- 4 year old

Learning Strengths

If the stages of a child's development are the framework for this temple, this house of faith we're building, then **Learning Strengths** are the wiring. **Learning Strengths** are factors that motivate a person to learn.

God has wired each person differently. Just as each person has favorite foods, each person also has favorite ways to learn, although she might not be conscious of it. These **Learning Strengths** make it easy for her to learn. They enable, energize, or even motivate her. She is comfortable on these paths of learning. Other paths, which may be preferred by another person, may be full of roadblocks for her.

Many researchers have studied the factors that affect the way we learn. The following information is a simplified overview of some of those models.

Sensory Strengths

Dr. Rita Dunn and Dr. Kenneth Dunn are educators who have done extensive research on learning styles. They found that people perceive information *best* when it comes to them through t h e sense they prefer: auditory, visual or tactile/kinesthetic.[1]

All preschoolers are **tactile/kinesthetic** They learn best when they are moving and active. But many older children learn best this way, too. Among all people over ten years old, 40% learn best by moving and doing.

Some children six through nine years old start showing a preference for **visual** learning. They learn best by seeing. Among all people over ten years old, 40% learn best by seeing.

Around ten years old, some children start showing a preference for **auditory** learning. They learn best by hearing. Among all people over ten years old, 20% learn best by hearing.[2]

What does this have to do with our teaching? We tend to teach the way we learn best. That means if we learn best by hearing, we tend to do most of our teaching by talking. We expect children to learn by just listening. If we learn best by seeing, we tend to use a lot of visuals. If we learn best by touching and doing, we tend to use lots of active learning.

Do you like to see charts, diagrams and maps? Do you like to watch a skill demonstrated before you try it? If your answer is yes, you are probably a visual learner and teacher.

Do you learn best by listening to teachers? Do you learn better if you hear yourself repeat the information? Do you like to learn by discussing issues with others? If your answer is yes, you are probably an auditory learner and teacher.

Do you learn best by trying things yourself? Do you like hands-on learning? Are you good at activities that require movement? If your answer is yes, you are probably a tactile/kinesthetic learner and teacher.

Think about how you learn best. Think about how you teach. Ask yourself if you need to move out of your comfort zone when you teach so you can communicate better to those children who learn differently than you do. If you are a visual learner and teacher, you would be wise to add auditory and tactile/kinesthetic activities to your lessons. If you are an auditory learner and teacher, you'd be wise to branch out into more visual and tactile/kinesthetic methods.

Physical and Environmental Strengths

Dunn and Dunn also discovered several environmental elements that affect learning.

Physical position. Some people learn best when they are lying flat on their stomachs. Some learn best when they are sprawled on a soft couch. Some concentrate best when they are sitting straight up.

Movement. Some people learn best when they are moving. In a traditional classroom setting, these people are constantly swinging a leg back and forth, or wiggling a foot, or drumming their fingers. I am a wiggler. When I have to concentrate, it helps if I pace the floor. I have learned to keep a pad of paper and pencil handy when I exercise, because when I begin moving, I get all kinds of ideas. Somehow when my body is moving, my mind is free to think.

Eating or chewing. What do these kids chew on in traditional classrooms where they can't have gum or snacks? They chew on their pencils and erasers, or even on scraps of paper. It helps them think.

Sound helps some people. Silence helps others. My sister used to come home from school and go into her room to do her homework. Then she would turn on loud rock music. I never believed that she was studying, because I prefer a quiet environment. But now I know my sister really was studying. She just does it differently than I do.

Light. Some people learn best in bright light. Some learn best in dim light. Most people learn best in natural daylight. My son's fourth grade teacher knew this. She talked her school into buying full spectrum light bulbs for her classroom. It gave the room the look of being lit by natural daylight. She said she could tell the difference in her students. They were more alert and learned more easily.

Temperature. Some people learn best when the temperature is cooler. Some learn best when it's warmer.

Time of day. Some people are morning people. Some are night people. Most elementary children learn best between 10 A.M. and 2 P.M.[3]

Design of the room. Some people learn best when they're in a formal setting with desks and chairs. But many learn best when they're in an informal setting. One interesting fact: It's easier for a person who prefers the formal setting to adapt to the informal setting than the other way around.[4]

Strengths in Style

Bernice McCarthy studied learning and found that there are four styles of learning.[5]

The **Imaginative** learner approaches what he must learn by asking the question, "Why?" He wants to know why the lesson is important. He learns best when he sees that it has meaning for his life. He also likes to work with people.

The **Analytic** learner asks, "What?" He wants to know facts. He likes things organized. He likes to solve problems and find answers. He's a thinker.

The **Common Sense** learner asks, "How?" He likes to test the theories and try ideas. He enjoys hands-on projects.

The **Dynamic** learner asks, "What can become of this?" He likes to brainstorm and try new things. He is creative and thinks toward the future.

Strengths in Intelligence

In his book *7 Kinds of Smart*, Thomas Armstrong explains Howard Gardner's theory of multiple intelligences. Gardner found that everyone has seven areas of intelligence. People usually operate well in two or three of the seven areas, although they can grow in the other areas as well.[6]

Linguistic. People who are intelligent in the area of linguistics enjoy playing with sounds and words. They learn best by saying, hearing and seeing words. Writing, reading, and listening are activities they enjoy.

Logical-Mathematical. People who operate well in the logical-mathematical area of intelligence enjoy exploring patterns and experimenting. Reasoning out problems is fun for them.

They enjoy science kits, brain teasers, computers, and things they can collect and categorize.

Spatial. Spatial people think in pictures. They are basically visual learners who enjoy films, videos, maps, cameras, building supplies and art materials.

Musical. Musical people like humming, singing, and playing instruments. They enjoy listening to music and are sensitive to rhythm and melody and all the sounds around them. Singing helps them memorize, and they often learn well when music is playing in the background.

Bodily-Kinesthetic. People who operate well in the bodily-kinesthetic area of intelligence like to learn through their senses. They enjoy anything physical. When they can touch and move, they learn more easily. They like role play, creative movement, and hands-on activities.

Interpersonal. These people like to organize and communicate. They enjoy other people and have lots of friends. Interacting with others helps them learn.

Intrapersonal. Intrapersonal people like to work alone. They are self-motivated and have deep thoughts, ideas and dreams.[7]

Motivational Forces

A recent book by educator Richard Lavoie entitled *The Motivational Breakthrough* describes in great detail the problems of unmotivated children and suggests specific ways teachers and parents can motivate them. Lavoie found that each person is inspired by a combination of more or less of each of the following forces.

Gregariousness. Motivated by belonging. Gregarious kids tend to be verbal, popular, and positive. They love being in groups.

Autonomy. Motivated by independence. Autonomy-driven kids are also usually verbal. They are curious, self-motivated, and enjoy working alone.

Status. Motivated by being important. Status-seekers tend to be self-critical and need reassurance. While they like to be in the spotlight, they don't want to fail and are sensitive to criticism. So they tend to comply.

Inquisitiveness. Motivated by knowing. Inquisitive kids like to problem-solve, experiment, read, and ask questions.

Aggression. Motivated by asserting themselves. Aggressive kids like responsibility. They speak out and may question authority or express strong opinions and complaints.

Power. Motivated by control. Power-charged kids can be leaders, competitive, courageous, persistent, and self-confident.

Recognition. Motivated by acknowledgment. Recognition-loving kids respond well to goals and performance. They're competitive, but also sensitive.

Affiliation. Motivated by associating. Affiliators like role models and adult attention. They are afraid of rejection, but they are usually helpful and often volunteer.[8]

Making it Practical

You may be sighing and rolling your eyes by now. How does all this information apply to my class? How in the world can we make our classrooms appeal to all these different kinds of learners?

First, know that you are not expected to be able to list all these styles and motivators. Nor is it necessary for you to know exactly which fits each child. In fact, it would not be wise to try to label each of your students to fit each of them into some sort of box. The point is to realize how unique each child is and know that we should provide our students VARIETY and FLEXIBILITY. We should include some activities to see, some to hear, and some to touch and do. We use music and puzzles, DVDs and role play. We try to be sensitive to children who like to work in groups and sensitive to children who enjoy working alone. Children are usually willing and able to do activities that don't match their specific learning preference, if they know that sooner or later they'll get to do something that appeals to them.

Here's how this information became practical to me. When my class had group time, we sat on a rug. A few children always preferred to lie on their stomachs or lean back. Since I knew that not all children learn best sitting up straight, I allowed them to sit any way they wanted as long as they did not disturb anyone else.

Sometimes I lowered the light level by telling the Bible story with the ceiling lights off, using flashlights or flickering fake candles. We often had a cooking activity and talked about the story or theme while the children ate. We sometimes played a tape softly as background music. We mixed active times with quiet times. I tried to be flexible and flow with what I perceived the students' needs to be, and I tried to include everyone by using variety. Now that I write curricula, I pay attention to making sure I provide plenty of variety and flexibility for other classrooms as well.

Every child is smart. Every child can learn.

One mother told me that her older son was very strong in the linguistic and logical-mathematical area. He made very good grades in school. Her younger son was not strong in those same areas and did not make good grades. But he was very strong in the tactile-kinesthetic area. He could catch and throw any kind of ball. Fortunately, this mother had learned about the theory of multiple intelligence. She would not allow her son to buy into the typical belief that the linguistic son was smarter than the kinesthetic son. She insisted that they see each other as smart, each with a strength in a different area. Accepting the fact that each child in our household or classroom is unique helps us respect and encourage every child.

Every child is smart. Every child can learn. It is we who must communicate in ways that help them understand. As Richard Lavoie wrote, "Basically, if the child cannot learn in the way we teach, we must teach in the way he learns."[9]

Chapter 13

Making the Connection

Lively Lessons

A teacher of two-year-olds
was teaching them how to pray.
She would say a phrase, and they would echo her.
At the end of the prayer, she said, "Awh-men."
All the children said, "Awh-men."
Then one little girl said, "And no women."

Turning on the Light

Learning occurs when experience touches truth. Mommy says, "Keep your hand away from the oven door. The oven is hot." That is a truth. What happens when the child touches the oven door? He has an experience. He learns a truth: The oven is hot.

But there are some truths we don't want children to experience. We want them to believe us when we tell them it's dangerous to cross a busy street by themselves. We hope they trust us when we say drugs will damage their bodies and minds. We don't want them to experience truths in areas that would be destructive to them. So we rely on the relationship of trust we've built with children. My father used to say, "A wise man learns from experience. A wiser man learns from someone else's experience." So sometimes we back up our instructions with stories in hopes that our children will learn from someone else's experience. We do the same as we teach spiritual concepts. We use stories, which we'll discuss in the next chapter, and we use experiences that touch the truth we want to teach.

What is an experience? It's something that happens to us involving our senses: sight, hearing, smell, taste, touch. The more of the five senses we involve, the stronger the experience and the memory of it will be. Let's look at how an expert taught using experience.

The Master Teacher

"Jesus was walking by Lake Galilee. He saw two brothers, Simon (called Peter) and Simon's brother Andrew. The brothers were fishermen, and they were fishing in the lake with a net. Jesus said, 'Come follow me. I will make you fishermen for men'" (Matthew 4:18,19, ICB).

What did Jesus do? He used a sensory experience to teach a truth. What kind of experience did Peter and Andrew have? They could **see** the sparkling waves of water and the wiggling fish. They could **hear** the waves sloshing, smacking the sides of the boat. They could **feel** the rough nets and the wet fish they tossed into the boat. They could **s m e l l** the fish. All this was part of their experience that day. Jesus simply wove a truth into their experience. He said, "From now on you can **fish** for men." He could have said, "Follow me, and I will show you how to win souls for God's kingdom." Instead, he linked truth to experience.

Do you suppose that on other occasions when Peter and Andrew saw those same sights and smelled those same smells, their minds went back to the memory of what Jesus said? Their experience had touched the truth Jesus was teaching. To say it another way, Jesus taught toward their experience.

On another occasion, Jesus told his followers, "Look at the birds. They don't plant or harvest or store food in barns. But your heavenly Father feeds the birds. And you know that you are worth much more than the birds. You cannot add any time to your life by worrying about it. And why do you worry about clothes? Look at the flowers in the field. See how they grow. They don't work or make clothes for themselves. But I tell you that even Solomon with his riches was not dressed as beautifully as one of these  flowers ... so you can be even more sure that God will clothe you" (Matthew 6:26-30, ICB).

Jesus taught the truth of God's care while his followers experienced nature. They could **see** and **hear** the birds. They could **smell** and **touch** the flowers. Their experience touched the truth Jesus was teaching. He taught toward their experience.

One day, Jesus was traveling through Samaria. He was tired, so he sat down beside a well. It wasn't long until a Samaritan woman came to the well to get water. Jesus asked her for a drink. The woman was surprised. "How can you ask me for a drink?" she said.

"You don't know who asked you for a drink," said Jesus. "If you knew, you would have asked me, and I would have given you living water" (John 4:10, ICB).

Why didn't Jesus say, "I am the bread of life?" Because she wasn't having an experience with bread. She was having an experience with water. She could **smell** the dank, wet well. She could **hear** the splash of her jar dropping into the water. She could **hear** the water dripping as she pulled the jar up. She could **feel** the water on her hands. She could **see** it slosh from side to side in the jar. She probably **tasted** some of it to quench her thirst. Jesus used her experience to teach His truth. When her experience touched His truth, she learned. How many times would she go to the well again, draw water, and think about "living water"?

In the previous examples, we saw Jesus using experiences that occurred naturally. But in Matthew 18:2-4, Jesus created an experience for His followers. "Jesus called a little child to him. He stood the child before the followers. Then he said, 'I tell you the truth. You must change and become like little children. If you don't do this, you will never enter the kingdom of heaven. The greatest person in the kingdom of heaven is the one who makes himself humble like this child'" (ICB). Jesus' followers could **see**, **hear** and **touch** the child. Their experience touched the truth Jesus was teaching. He created the experience and taught toward it.

Perhaps my favorite example of all is in John 13. "It was almost time for the Jewish Passover Feast... during the meal Jesus stood up and took off his outer clothing. Taking a towel, he wrapped it around his waist. Then he poured water into a bowl and began to wash the followers' feet. He dried them with the towel that was wrapped around him." Jesus created another experience for his disciples. They **saw** him kneel with the towel around his waist. They **felt** the cool, wet, cleansing water. They **felt** the towel massage their tired feet. They **heard** the water drip back into the bowl. With this experience, Jesus taught them about servanthood. "I did this as an example for you. So you should do as I have done for you" (John 13:15, ICB).

How It's Done

Linking truth to a child's experience is easiest to do in the process of parenting. That's because the experiences come naturally. You can do what God told his people to do long ago. "These commandments that I give you today are to be upon your hearts. Impress them on your children. Talk about them when you sit at home and when you walk along the road, when you lie down and when you get up" (Deuteronomy 6:6,7). You can take the experiences that happen every day and link God's truths to them. There are three steps involved.

1) The experience.

2) The truth.

3) The challenge.

For example, you and your child hear thunder. That's the experience. You teach a truth toward that experience by saying, "The Bible tells about a time when people thought they heard thunder, but it was really God talking." (See John 12:29.) Then you challenge the child to think about God: "What do you think God's voice sounds like? How does God speak to us? How do we speak to God?"

In the classroom, we do this procedure a bit differently. We create experiences to which we link the truth we want to teach. These experiences are called activities. We teach toward the experience children have during the activities. The same three steps are involved: 1) Experience, 2) Truth, 3) Challenge.

For example, let's say we want to teach preschoolers about sharing. Our story is about Abraham who shared food with three visitors. So we create an experience: eating and sharing apples. We give every other child two apple slices. That leaves half the group without apples. We ask each child to share with the child sitting beside him. That's the experience. While the children are having this experience, we tell them the point we want to get across, the truth we want to teach: "Abraham shared.

God is happy when we share." Then we challenge the children further by asking leading questions: "How do you feel when someone shares with you? Why is sharing a loving thing to do? Why does God want us to share? Is it always easy to share?" We guide children's thoughts and conversation during or immediately after the activity. In a lesson plan, this may be called "Discussion" or "Guided Conversation" or "To Talk About."

With an older class, the experience might be passing around anise seed and asking each student to take a pinch and chew it. As they chew on the anise seed, you tell them that people in Jesus' time had no toothbrushes or toothpaste. They often chewed anise seed to sweeten their breath. So when Mary and Joseph made the trip to Bethlehem, they may have packed a small bag of anise seed, in the same way you would pack your toothbrush and toothpaste.

One very important area of active learning is works of service. Children can serve in a variety of very real, meaningful ways. They can collect food and make food baskets to take to needy families. They can visit homes of the elderly. They can help rake leaves and mow lawns. Older children can help teach younger children's classes. There are dozens of ways they can serve. They learn as they serve and in the process, they gain a sense of belonging and competence.

After Jesus washed his disciples' feet, he told them to serve others. To **do** what they had learned. An old Chinese proverb says, "What I hear, I forget. What I see, I remember. What I do, I know." Jesus said, "You should do as I have done for you." A few verses later, he says, "If you know these things, you will be happy if you do them." Jesus' disciples experienced his lesson with their senses. They heard Jesus' truth. Now they needed to **do**. That is learning.

Your Map

How did you come to be a teacher? Here's what often happens. The call goes out at church: There's a need for teachers. You volunteer. Then in a group meeting, or maybe just a spontaneous "meet-you-in-the-hall" connection with the supervisor, you are handed a booklet and/or a large envelope or box. This is your lesson plan book, a packet of "visuals," and maybe a booklet of "handwork." Sometimes the material includes a box of toys.

Where do you go from here? First of all, let's take a look at your lesson plan book. It's part of the curriculum your church ordered. What is curriculum? It's a map. It tells you how to get where you want to go. It will have overall goals for your age group. Through the year, the lessons will take you toward that goal. Lessons are the points of interest you pass as you travel the route on the "map." Each lesson you pass puts you one step nearer your overall goal. In fact, each of these interest points (or lesson plans) has goals of its own that fit into the bigger picture.

However, lesson plans are simply suggestions for what to do during class time. Not having a lesson plan is very likely to frustrate you. You will have a hard time reaching your goal without a plan. But being glued or locked-in to your lesson plan will likely make you just as frustrated, because the people who write lesson plans cannot know your specific situation. Your situation is different from mine. Plus, your situation may change from year to year.

I used the same curriculum, the same lesson plans, for eight years. Each year was different. One year I had twelve children in my class. The next year I had twenty-eight. One year my students included several foreign children. Another year I had a child in a wheelchair. One year the kids listened eagerly at group time. The next year, they were into rough-and-tumble wrestling instead of listening. I've taught in tiny classrooms and huge classrooms, in churches with few materials and in churches with resource centers where workers had my requested materials stacked and ready to go when I dropped by before class. I've taught in situations where I had only 45 minutes to complete the activities, and I've taught in classes where I had 90 minutes.

Can one lesson plan cover all these possibilities? No. That's why a lesson plan is a group of suggestions for you. When you get your lesson plan, read it and ask yourself some questions:

1. Does this fit my class needs?
2. Does this fit the time schedule I have?
3. Does this fit the materials available to me?
4. Does this fit the abilities and interests of my children?
5. Does this fit the space available to me?

Delete or add activities according to your answers to these questions.

How do you find activities to add? You need resource books. Good activity books broaden your choices. You may also think of some activities on your own. Avoid coloring books and lick-and-stick "handwork" since these require no original thinking, and everyone's pictures look just alike. If you are really going to be child-sensitive, you'll opt for more original arts and crafts as well as other types of activities.

Use visual teaching-aid pictures sparingly. There are many more active, interesting and fun ways to involve children in the lesson. The last thing you want to do is bore the children. God is not boring. Life in Him is an adventure. So learning about Him should be an adventure too.

If you are excited about what's going on in class, chances are the children will be excited too. If you're bored with it, chances are they'll be bored too. Ask, "How can I use my special gifts and talents to enhance this lesson? How can I make it exciting?" For example, if you're a good cook, you could do a cooking activity with the students. If you're a gardener, you might bring flowers to examine or seedlings to plant. What do you have that would help communicate the theme of the lesson?

As you think about the activities you need, remember to "Take AIM." Make your lessons

Age-appropriate

Interesting

Meaningful

Children want to be where the action is. Where the excitement is. Where it matters. Where you care. And they know you care when you spend the time to help them enjoy the lesson through age-appropriate, interesting, meaningful activities.

Chapter 14

The Five-Day Sandwich

Telling Bible Stories Creatively

A young boy listened as his teacher told the story of the Good Samaritan. When a character passed by the hurt man, she made the hurt man call, "Help!"But with each person who passed, the "Help!" got softer and weaker until the man's cries could hardly be heard. After church, the boy's mother asked him what he had learned in class. The boy said, "I learned that you gotta' call for help louder than that!"

Who Tells the Stories?

There's a story told about a wealthy traveler who went on an African adventure tour. One day, his tour took him to a remote tribal village where there was no electricity. The wealthy traveler felt sorry for the people who lived in the village, so he paid to have electricity brought to the village, and he shipped a television set to every hut.

A few years later, the wealthy traveler had an opportunity to visit this same village again. To his surprise, he found all the television sets piled into one large hut.

He asked the head man, "Why do you not use your televisions?"

The head man answered, "Because we have a storyteller."

"But TV knows thousands of stories," said the traveler.

"That's true," said the head man. "But the storyteller knows us."

George Gerbner, a researcher of the role of media in our culture, says, "Whoever tells the stories controls how children grow up... Television now tells most of the stories."[1] That may be true, but there is still a tremendous attraction to the storyteller in person, as the legend of the African tribe illustrates. Jim Trelease, author of *The Read-Aloud Handbook*, writes, "If a plastic box in your living room can turn on your child to chocolate breakfast cereal, then you should be able to do ten times as much—because you are a sensitive, loving, and caring human being."[2]

Stories are powerful. Storytelling is powerful. Yet the Bible story is often the most overlooked and ho-hum part of the Sunday school hour. One well-worn technique of storytelling in Sunday school is for the teacher to read the story aloud from the teacher's guide, which is on her lap in front of her. Meanwhile, she moves figures on a flannel board according to the instructions she's reading. It's no wonder children get restless and bored. If you use this technique, realize that this is a starting point. Grow and move on from there.

Dr. Howard Hendricks, author of *The 7 Laws of the Teacher*, writes, "We teach Bible stories as if the people were cardboard characters who had none of the feelings, thoughts and problems we do."[3] Robert Coles, author of *The Spiritual Life of Children*, was asked why he says biblical stories aren't always interesting to young people today. His answer was, "Because they're not presented as stories by and about human beings. They're abstracted and presented in an unreal world in which religion equals some kind of Sunday-at-11 duty and obligation. . . . If the story is told with conviction and aimed at their hearts, they'll listen."[4]

Our Heritage of Story

Storytelling is breathing life into characters. What God did literally, the storyteller does figuratively. "And the Lord God formed man from the dust of the ground and breathed into his nostrils the breath of life, and man became a living being" (Genesis 2:7). We make people come alive in the child's mind, in his imagination.

Why? Peninnah Schram, a Jewish storyteller, puts it this way: "When a generation can feel its ancestors' feelings, share their ideas and sorrows, the lessons of their lives will live on."[5] Many cultures, including the Jewish culture, have preserved a body of stories, handed down from generation to generation. These stories serve to give people a cultural sense of heritage. These are their roots.

Storytelling is a shared experience. The storyteller is a tour guide, taking listeners on a tour of the story. In our case, the story is God's story, our heritage, our roots, the truth of how God deals with his people. It's the perfect blend of knowing Bible facts and learning how God works in our daily lives. That's all the more reason to make the story exciting for the listeners.

Amat Victoria Curam

The Latin expression "Amat Victoria Curam" means "Victory Loves Preparation." If you are going to have success in the classroom, you must prepare. When Jack Maguire, a professional storyteller, teaches people to tell stories, he takes them through five steps.[6] I've taken these steps a bit further and have made them into what I call a Five-Day Sandwich.

To build the Five-Day Sandwich, you add one ingredient each day for five days. Since there are seven days in a week, you have five days to "build the sandwich," and one day to teach the story. That leaves one day of "grace," so that you have room to forget, or to be too busy, or too tired, or whatever else comes up.

All you need is five or ten minutes a day to build this sandwich, although you can spend longer if you'd like. Try to work this into your regular schedule, doing it at the same time each day. Any time is fine. My best time is the ten minutes at night just before going to bed.

Begin learning next week's story on the day after you have taught. For example, if you teach on Sunday, look at next week's lesson plan on Monday. Try to start learning the story for next week. This gives you an entire week to think about what you might do during your next lesson. For example, as you read the next lesson, let's say you think of a wonderful activity you could do. It requires balloons. You now have time to get balloons at the store. If you had kept the lesson book closed until Saturday night, you wouldn't have had time. Or you may be in the grocery store, passing the bin of oranges. "Hey!" you think. "I could use a couple of these for next week's lesson." If you don't know what the lesson is for next week, opportunities like this can't happen.

Now let's build that sandwich!

1. Enjoy

The meat is the story itself. So on the first day, read the story for your next lesson from the Bible. Read it simply to *ENJOY* it and relate it to your life. Does it have a meaning for you? Does God want to tell you something from this passage?

2. Character

This is the cheese on our sandwich, which you will add as you read the passage again the second day. In this reading, take a good look at each main *CHARACTER*. Close your eyes. What do you think this character looked like? If you were with him on this occasion, what would his voice sound like? If you shook hands with him, what would his handshake feel like? How would he walk? Does he have a smell about him? Practice this now with the story of David and Goliath. David's handshake would certainly be different from Goliath's.

Of course, you won't go into the classroom and tell the children, "David was 5'10". He had wavy brown hair and dark brown eyes." You won't fictionalize. You will tell only the facts as the Bible tells them. The point is for you to start thinking of the characters as real flesh and blood people. Because they were. If you can start feeling that they were real, you will tell your stories with more excitement. You will be animated about it. You will tell the story as if the characters were real living, breathing people in a real hot and cold, up and down, quiet and noisy world.

You might try doing some of these exercises with your students in class sometimes. Ask them to imagine what David might have been like. Ask them what they think Goliath looked like. This will help them think of these characters as the real people they were.

3. Phrases

Here is the onion to put on the sandwich. You will read the same passage the third day, this time reading for any *PHRASE* that you might need to memorize. Your aim is not to memorize the story word for word, but to retell it in your own 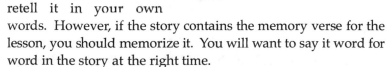 words. However, if the story contains the memory verse for the lesson, you should memorize it. You will want to say it word for word in the story at the right time.

In some stories you'll find special phrases that give the story a spark. You should also memorize these. For example, in the story of David and Goliath, I would memorize what David said to Goliath. "You come against me with a spear and a sword, but I come against you in the name of the Lord." This is a powerful part of the story.

Another example is a very simple phrase that appears in the story of Gideon. His small army surrounds the enemy. It's night. Everyone is watching Gideon and waiting... waiting... waiting. At last Gideon blows his trumpet, breaks his pitcher, and holds up his torch. The soldiers also blow their trumpets, break their pitchers, and hold their torches high. Then they shout, "A sword for the Lord and for Gideon!" I yell this phrase right there in the classroom. It makes everyone want to jump up and shout, "Yes! Hurray for Gideon!" It's exciting. As it should be.

4. Environment

This is the tomato for your sandwich. As you read the same passage on the fourth day, pay attention to the *ENVIRONMENT*, the setting of the story. Occasionally the biblical account tells what the weather was like. The previous example of Abraham showed him sitting outside on a hot day. His tent was near the trees of Mamre. So we know there were trees, there was a tent, and it was a hot day.

But often we are not told much about the environment. So again, close your eyes. What do you think it was like? Is the landscape rocky, sandy, forested, a meadow? Is there a lake or pond or ocean? Imagine yourself there. What do you see? What do you hear? Birds? Wind? Thunder? A brook? An army? A crowd of people coming down the road? What do you smell? Do you smell the dinner that Martha is cooking – or fish the disciples caught? What is the weather and the temperature?

Again, you will not tell children something that is not fact. But you can make it real to yourself so that the telling will be believable.

5. Total

Now put the lettuce on the sandwich. On the fifth day, read through the story passage again. You will probably enjoy it more than you did the first time you read it, because you have made it seem real. And it *was* real once upon a time. It happened to real people in a real place, just as real as where you are right now.

The key to successful storytelling is believability. Make it believable. Be excited to share this story. Remember: if you're not excited, the children won't be excited.

6. Prayer

But something is missing from this sandwich. What is it? We have meat, cheese, onion, tomato and lettuce. We need bread. Surround all the steps with *PRAYER*. Pray before you begin. Pray after you've finished. And why not go ahead and pile this sandwich high? Pray in between, too. Let the Lord guide your preparation and touch your own heart with what He wants you to glean from this passage.

A Story a Day

If you teach in a school setting or day care in which you tell one story a day, you can still prepare using some of the 5-Day Sandwich principles. At some point as you prepare for the next day's story, read the passage and think for five to ten minutes about the character and setting. Try to think of it as a real happening so that when you tell the story, you'll express the energy of the event.

Four Storytelling Tools You Carry Everywhere

As far as the delivery of the story goes, you have four useful tools that you carry with you no matter where you are:

1) Gestures

Use your hands and body language to reinforce your words. For example, you not only say, "She had a little baby," you also hold your arms as if cradling a baby, rocking back and forth.

2) Tone of Voice

You can yell, as I do in the story of Gideon. (Practice at home when no one's around.) Or you can whisper loudly. I do this when I'm telling something that happens at night. Or maybe you want to create a suspenseful mood. Lower your voice. The children will get as quiet as they can in order to hear you.

You can also speak slowly. I do this when I tell about Abraham sitting outside his tent on a very hot day. If it's a very hot day, nobody is moving very fast. Or you can speak very quickly. Do this when someone is running or riding in a chariot. Maybe there's a storm, and you want to build tension by speaking urgently.

You can make the pitch of your voice go up if someone is climbing up a tree or going up a mountain. You can start high and make your voice go lower if someone is coming down a mountain. Try some different skills with your voice and incorporate them into your storytelling.

3) Response

Children will have a natural response to your story. You can adjust your storytelling according to their response. If they look like they don't understand, explain. If they look like they're losing interest, get more animated and move on to the next part of the story. If they look overwhelmed or frightened, lighten up on the dramatics.

4) Words

Know the ages of the children to whom you will be telling the story. Take into consideration the words they can understand. Remember: Preschool children don't understand symbolism and will take you literally.

Story Material

Storytelling purists say the only way to be true to real storytelling tradition is to tell the story without any props, using only your voice and body movements. You can do that, of course, but it's usually not necessary. There are many kinds of materials that can help you tell stories. So as you plan the story, think of the materials available to you.

You can use the traditional flannel figures. These are always good for children to use to retell the story themselves later in the class time. But be careful not to use flannel figures all the time.

Vary the materials you use from week to week, so children always wonder what exciting and fun things you have planned for them today. If they seem bored with one method, don't use it. Opt for something else.

Puppets are fun. They can be store-bought, or homemade. One easy way to make hand puppets is to staple two paper plates together and draw a face on one side. Insert your hand between the two plates. Your wrist becomes the neck of the puppet.

You can also use **story pictures**. The smaller the group, the more intricate and detailed the picture can be. For larger groups, simpler, bold pictures are better so everyone can see. But be careful. It's easy to get in the habit of relying on flannel figures and story pictures. A steady diet of these becomes dull. There are so many other exciting ways to get students into the story actively that you may never even need flannel figures and story pictures. The important thing is to choose methods you can get excited about.

You can use **blocks** or **boxes**. Let children build the houses or the tower or the city that you will use when telling the story. Try using children's toy figures to represent Bible characters. Tell the story in a box of sand, or if the setting is on a lake, tell it with figures in a tub of water.

Children usually enjoy **acting out** the story. Let them dress up in old sheets, towels and pillowcases with arm holes cut in them. For younger children, it helps if the teacher narrates and moves the children around where she wants them to stand. Blue sheets can be large rivers or seas. Pitch a **tent** in the room when you tell stories of Abraham or the Israelites in the desert. Bring **stuffed animals** to help tell the story of Noah or the story of Creation.

Baby powder is a fun addition to your storytelling kit. Sprinkle some baby powder on children's arms to represent leprosy. When the "lepers" are made well, let children rub their arms to rub off the powder.

Stories for Older Children

Let older students draw a mural "backdrop" to set the stage for the story. Let them look up geographical and historical details. Find out what's happening in that part of the world today. For these story-related activities, teachers may need to be resource people, finding and providing these details at one or more "information stations."

One interesting possibility for story exploration for older students is to set up a "Jigsaw" classroom. This term was coined by educator Eliot Aronson for use in his public school classrooms. But the concept can be used to study the Bible, too. Children are divided into groups, three or four students to a group. Each group is like a separate jigsaw puzzle, with each member of the group being one of the puzzle pieces. Each member becomes a reporter and is given a different assignment. For example, the first member of each group tries to find out what happened to Paul in Lystra and Derbe. Another member of the group finds out where these cities would be located on a globe today. The third child finds out what kind of transportation they had in those days. A fourth could find out about the climate.

You provide the resources for the students to use in research. These resources could be simple information pages that you have posted at different parts of the room. You give the children time to accomplish their assignments. Then they meet back in their original group (the "jigsaw" puzzle comes together). The students then teach each other within their groups, reporting on what they discovered.

Older students can also:
- publish a newspaper with Bible stories written as if they were current events
- write a commercial for the story
- act out the story and make a visual recording
- narrate the story for an audio recording, using different voices and sound effects
- write letters about the story to one of the story's characters

- write a journal as if they were traveling with the story character
- write or tell a sequel to the story
- practice telling the story, then go to a younger classroom and tell the story there

The difficulty in telling Bible stories is that many of the children have heard them again and again. Finding new and interesting ways to tell these wonderful stories is a challenge. Or consider telling Bible stories that the students have not yet heard. Jesus said, "Every teacher... who has been instructed about the kingdom of heaven is like the owner of a house who brings out of his storeroom new treasures as well as old" (Matthew 13:52). New stories as well as fresh approaches to classic stories keep students interested.

Remember, we don't tell the story for the story's sake alone. We tell the story to see in it a truth that is relevant to the child's life. As one pastor said, "The Bible is not for information, but transformation." Get to the issues that affect the children you are teaching. Then let the students discuss these real life issues.

Chapter 15

Keep it in Mind
Scripture Memory

---

*A four-year old came out of Sunday school
saying his memory verse, "Children obey your carrots."*

What's a Memory?

In one of my favorite picture books, *Wilfrid Gordon McDonald Partridge* by Mem Fox, Wilfrid Gordon's best friend at the old people's home has lost her memory. Being quite young, Wilfrid doesn't understand. So he asks all his friends at the old people's home, "What's a memory?" Each person he asks tells him something different.[1]

What is a memory?

Scientists tell us memory involves chemical and physical changes in nerve cells in the brain. Memory is centered in the cerebral cortex, which controls functions like problem-solving and language. By the time a child is three years old, his brain is 75-80% of its adult size. But he's growing quickly. By the time he's four, his brain is 90% of its adult size. This means there are more connections between parts of the brain. More connections mean increased alertness, attention and memory.

From a psychologist's perspective, there are basically three kinds of memory. First, there's sensory memory. This comes to you through one or more of your senses. But sensory memory is held in your mind for only an instant after you experience it. Then it's gone.

The second kind of memory is short-term memory. This is the kind of memory you hold in your mind as long as you are actively thinking about it. For example, you look up a phone number and repeat it to yourself as you enter the number. By the time you've finished your conversation and hung up, you've forgotten the number. It lasts in your mind only about 20 seconds.

The third kind of memory is long-term memory. This kind of memory can last the rest of your life. One way something enters long-term memory is by intense emotion. I don't remember much about my life before I turned five. But I do remember vividly two events. I remember dropping a milk bottle on my toe. (This was in the "olden" days of glass milk bottles.) And I remember sitting on my porch with my grandmother when yellow jackets were buzzing around. The first event was planted in my long-term memory because of pain. The second entered because of fear.

Another way something can get into long-term memory is by repetition. Did you ever move to a new town? When you drove to church or the ball park or the mall for the first time, you may have had to follow a map. You had to read street signs and look for landmarks. But you drove that route over and over again. Then one day, you left your house, and the next thing you knew you were at your destination. You had no memory of having driven the correct streets to get there. The repetition of driving that route had stored it in your long-term memory.

Much of our learning from birth throughout our lives comes from repetition. We do something so often that it becomes automatic to us. But there is another kind of repetition: rote memory. Rote memory is defined as mindless repetition done mechanically or without understanding. This is the kind of repetition students often do in school. They memorize information to make a good grade on the test but forget it as soon as the test is over. We might even call this mid-term memory, because it's longer than short-term memory, but shorter than long-term memory. We hold onto the information as long as it serves a purpose. When it ceases to serve the purpose, we drop it.

Did you memorize the states of the U.S. and their capitals when you were in school? Did you memorize the Presidents of the United States? Did you memorize the Gettysburg address or the Preamble to the U.S. Constitution? Do you remember all of them? Or did you forget? Why?

Try another experiment. How many scriptures did you memorize as you grew up? How many can you say now? Why do you remember the ones you remember?

Why Teach Memory Verses?

When we see how many Bible verses we memorized and how few we remember, we might ask why we should memorize scriptures at all. We might especially ask that question if we had difficulty memorizing, or if we never got the prize, or if the teacher or class put us down when we failed to learn the scripture for the day. But there are some important reasons to memorize scripture.

1. Meditation

David was called "a man after God's own heart" (1 Samuel 13:14). How was he able to come so close to God? I think we find one of the reasons in Psalm 145:5. David said, "I will meditate on your wonderful works." In Psalm 143:5, David said, "I remember the days of long ago; I meditate on all your works and consider what your hands have done. I spread out my hands to you; my soul thirsts for you like a parched land." David was serious about seeking God.

Meditating on scripture means deliberately and consciously considering it. It's turning the words over and over in your thoughts, pouring through it, "bathing" in it. It's much easier to do when the words are already in your heart, or you are in the process of putting them into your heart. Psalm 119 is full of verses about meditating on God's precepts, decrees and promises.

2. Fighting Temptation

Psalm 119 gives us another reason to memorize scripture: to fight temptation. Verse 11 says, "I have hidden your word in my heart that I might not sin against you." Ephesians 6:17 tells us that God's word is the sword of the Spirit. Luke 4 shows how Jesus used this sword to fight temptation. When the devil tempted Jesus, He fought back by quoting scripture. If Jesus did it, maybe we should too. Children can be equipped to fight temptation the way Jesus did.[2]

3. Prayer

A third reason to memorize scripture is to use it in prayer. 1 John 5:14,15 says, "This is the confidence we have in approaching God: that if we ask anything according to his will, he hears us. And if we know that he hears us – whatever we ask – we know that we have what we asked of him." How do we know we are asking according to His will? One of the surest ways is to pray scripture. "Lord, you are my shepherd. I shall lack nothing. Make me lie down in green pastures. Lead me beside quiet waters. Restore my soul" (Psalm 23).

4. Guidance

Another reason to memorize scripture is so we can rely on it during life's experiences. There was a quiet, shy boy in one of my four-year-old classes. We had been memorizing the verse, "I know that God can do all things" (Job 42:2). One evening his mother peeked into the classroom before class started. She said, "Today Timothy came up to me, pointed to the sky and said, 'Mommy, I know that God up there can do all things.'" The verse had jumped out of the classroom and had found its way into his everyday life.

Another little girl in my class was playing at home with her two year old sister. They were in the yard, and a bee flew near. Her little sister ran into the house crying, afraid of the bee. The big sister ran in after her, calling, "Remember: In God I trust, I will not be afraid" (Psalm 56:11). She was applying her memory verse to a life experience.

One pastor tells the story of his grown daughter who had run away from home and gotten into drugs and worse. At the lowest point in her life, she found herself in a run-down trailer, hungry and friendless. She lay in bed all day. But a memory verse she had learned in Sunday school when she was four years old kept running through her mind. God used that verse to take her back home where she started a new life in the Lord.

So the question is not, "*Should* we memorize scripture?" The question is, "*How* should we memorize scripture so that we can really remember it?"

Keys to Memorization

As teachers, we usually expect children to memorize without teaching them how. We just say, "Here's your memory verse for next week. Be sure to learn it." We may even add, "so you get your prize." But if we really think memorizing scripture is important, we will help children learn how to do it.

1. Focus.

The first thing anyone must do to memorize something is to focus on it, to think about it. It's important to spend some of your class time focusing on the verse.

2. Link it to something children already know.

Ask yourself how this verse relates to the children. What do they know that you can link it to? For example, "I know that God can do all things." How does that relate to a four-year-old? The key is in the word "do." What is a four-year-old able to do? What is he not able to do? A four year old's world consists of what he can do and can't do. God is able to do anything.

3. Help children understand what they are memorizing.

Frank Smith, in his book *Insult to Intelligence* says, "Rote memorization is the worst strategy for trying to learn anything we do not understand... Learning by rote is the hardest and most pointless way to learn. Students who use memorized formulas without understanding commit monumental mistakes without suspecting their errors."[3] If children are going to memorize, they must understand what they're memorizing.

I once taught the verse, "Be quick to listen and slow to speak" (James 1:19) to a group of five-year-olds. I thought it was a simple verse. But while I was listening to the children repeat the verse, it occurred to me that they didn't understand it. So I asked them what the verse meant. They said it meant, "T-a-l-k r-e-a-l s-l-o-w." Needless to say, I had some explaining to do.

Remember that children who are under six or seven years old do not understand symbolism. Before presenting a memory verse to children, ask yourself if you think they will understand it. Many Bible verses contain symbolic language. Children will find it easier to memorize these verses if you discuss them first and clear up any misunderstandings.

4. Make it relevant to the child.

We remember concepts and facts that we use often. They are relevant to us. I remember lots of grammar rules, because I use them every day when I write and speak. But I don't remember theories about geometry. I never need them, so I never use them. Make sure the verses you teach relate to your students' lives.

For the young child, my philosophy is "remember a few rather than forget many." I choose only four to six verses for young children to learn for the entire year. I'd rather they leave my class knowing four verses well than learn a verse each week, none of which they remember after they move on.

In first through third grade, children should still have more oral memory work than written memory work, because many of them are still struggling with reading and writing. As they grow older, they can be expected to learn more verses.

What are some practical ways we can help children learn memory verses? Remember the three sensory areas in which people learn: auditory, visual, and tactile/kinesthetic. Try teaching the verse in an auditory way to help the auditory learner memorize it. Teach it in a visual way to help the visual learner. And teach it in a tactile/kinesthetic way to help the T-K learner.

Ideas for the Ears

Children who learn best by listening will be able to memorize by repeating the verse over and over again. They can learn from hearing themselves or someone else say it. It will help if each time you say the verse you use the same inflection and rhythm. For example, "I know... that God... can do ALL things." Say it the same way every time.

Sometimes it's fun to repeat the verse in different voices. Say it in a low voice. Say it in a high voice. Say it softly. Shout it. Say it in different foreign accents. Say it like you think a cat would talk. Or try getting faster and faster each time you repeat the verse, until you can't say it intelligibly anymore. Singing the memory verse may also help auditory learners. Perhaps you can make up a tune or put the words to a tune you already know. Or let the children put the verse to music.

If any of the students have watches that can be set to beep every hour on the hour, you might suggest that they set their watches for that function on a Saturday. Then every time their watch beeps, they say the verse.

Ideas for the Eyes

Visual learners memorize more easily if they can see something that will help them learn. Ask them to mentally visualize the words in the written verse. Or they might organize a verse that contains a list by putting the first letter of each word together to see what it spells. I learned Philippians 4:8 this way. I learned the words **TNR PLA EP** (tenor play E.P.) "Finally brothers, whatever is **T**rue, whatever is **N**oble, whatever is **R**ight, whatever is **P**ure, whatever is **L**ovely, whatever is **A**dmirable, if anything is **E**xcellent or worthy of **P**raise, think on these things."

Or try a simple game. Get some index cards and write one word of the verse on each card. Then lay out the cards in order. Read the verse aloud together. Then ask one child to pick any card and turn it face down. Read it together again, supplying the

133

missing word when you come to it. Ask another child to turn over any card. Read it again, this time saying both missing words. Keep going this way until all the cards are turned over and they are still "reading" the verse.

This same game can be done with sticky postable notes. Or use a chalk board or dry erase board, erasing one word at a time. Or instead of writing the words on cards, write them with a permanent marker on inflated balloons. To "erase" a word, the child must pop the balloon. You can furnish a pin for this, or you can tell the children to sit on the balloons to pop them.

Ideas for the Hands

Sometimes you can put hand motions to the verse. Our class did this with Deuteronomy 6:5: "Love the Lord with all your heart and soul and strength." When we said "love," we put our hands on our hearts. When we said, "Lord," we pointed up. When we said, "heart," hands went back over our hearts again. When we said, "strength," we made muscles with our upper arms like strong men.

Another fun way to be tactile/kinesthetic with memory work is to toss a beach ball. Whoever the ball is thrown to says the first word of the verse. He then throws the ball to another person who says the next word and so on until the entire verse has been quoted. A variation of this is for the child who catches the ball to say the whole verse, then throw it to another child who says the whole verse and so on.

You could write each word of the verse on an index card, then mix up the cards and ask the children to arrange them in order. A more active, fun way is to pin the cards on the backs of children and then ask one or two other children to arrange the "pinned" children in order. Or hang the scrambled cards on a clothesline that's been strung across the room. Or write the words on paper cups and form teams, seeing which team can arrange their cups in the proper verse order first.

There are also traditional games you can play using words of the verse. Make a hopscotch path with one word written in each square. Then play hopscotch, saying each word as the student hops on it. Or play London Bridge. The person who gets "caught" must say the verse. Or play Duck, Duck, Goose, but with each tap of the head, a word of the verse is said. On the last word of the verse, the one tapped chases the tapper to see who can get back to the empty spot first.

God's Reminders

As you can see, many of these ideas combine factors that appeal to auditory, visual, and T/K learners. The variations of what you can do are endless.

God uses all of these ways to help his people remember. He uses auditory methods. Exodus 17 tells about the time Joshua led God's people out to fight. Moses was watching from a mountain. When Moses held up his hands, God's people would win. Aaron and Hur ended up supporting Moses' hands when Moses got tired. Joshua and his army won. "Then the Lord said to Moses, 'Write this on a scroll as something to be remembered and make sure that Joshua *hears* it'" (Exodus 17:14). At one time, God told Moses to write down a song so the events would not be forgotten (Deuteronomy 31:19-22)

God also uses visual methods. He set the rainbow in the sky to remind Him never again to destroy the earth with water (Genesis 9:12-17). When the Israelites crossed the Jordan River, God told the people to take stones from the river bed and put them at their camp. God said, "These stones are to be a memorial to the people of Israel forever." When children asked about the stones, the people were to tell them about crossing the Jordan.

God uses tactile/kinesthetic methods. During the Feast of Booths the people were to make and live in booths for seven days to help them remember how they had wandered in the wilderness for forty years. For us, the wine and flat bread of the communion or Lord's supper, as well as the water of baptism, are tactile reminders of what Jesus did for us.

Chapter 16

An Ounce of Prevention
Discipline - Directing the Child

Four-year-old: "Daniel's grandmother died."

Mom: "How sad! Did you tell him you're sorry?"

Four-year-old: "I didn't do it!"

God's Discipline

Discipline means "discipling," making disciples or followers. I like the word "discipling," because it puts the focus on the teacher or parent. The goal of discipling someone is to help them grow to be like their teacher. This is a big responsibility. It starts with us. Do we want children to be like us? We must focus on ourselves first, because children will copy what we do and echo what we say.

Who disciplines us? God does. It makes sense, then, to look at how God disciplines us, His children, in order to discover how to discipline the children in our care.

"In our care" is the operative phrase. "The Lord disciplines those he loves" (Hebrews 12:6). He trains us in the ways of love. That's God's number one Kingdom Principle of Discipline: LOVE comes first. God's *commitment* to us shows His love. When the first man and woman disobeyed, God could have abandoned the entire human race. But He didn't. Love does not abandon. He said, "Never will I leave you; never will I forsake you" (Deuteronomy 31:6, Hebrews 13:5). God is committed to pursuing us. He continually invites us to have a personal Father-child relationship with Him.

However, although God never leaves us, His closeness to us is affected by our choices. "Your iniquities have separated you from your God; your sins have hidden his face from you" (Isaiah 59:2). God's number two Kingdom Principle of Discipline is:

SEPARATION is the result of wrong choices. When we follow God's way, we open ourselves to His close presence, but when we turn from God's way, we close ourselves to His close presence. "Come near to God and he will come near to you" (James 4:8). The primary consequence of turning from Him is a natural consequence: separation. When Adam and Eve disobeyed, they were separated from privileges they had previously enjoyed: the beautiful garden, abundant provision, God's close presence as He walked with them in the cool of the day. But we must keep one important truth in mind: Even though sin separates us from God's close presence, we are never separated from His love (Romans 8:38, 39).

God's number three Kingdom Principle of Discipline is: God always SHOWS THE WAY. He doesn't say just, "No. No. No." He give us "Yes." When God says, "Stop behaving this way," He says, "Behave this way instead." He gives us a vision for who we are as His children. "Put off falsehood... speak truthfully" (Ephesians 4:25). "You have taken off your old self with its practices and have put on the new self" (Colossians 3:9, 10).

In fact, God communicated His rules to us in order to show us the way. He created the world and knows how it works. Instead of leaving us on our own to figure it out, He told us how it's set up to work. Kindness works. If everyone were kind, life would work the way it's supposed to. Rudeness does not work. If everyone were rude, life wouldn't work.

But God didn't stop at simply communicating rules. He sent His Son to earth to show us that it's not outward rules that are the most important, it's the inward heart. "What's the most important rule?" a man asked Jesus. "Love the Lord your God with all your heart and with all your soul and with all your strength and with all your mind; and, Love your neighbor as yourself," answered Jesus, echoing God's early instructions to His people (Deuteronomy 6:5, Luke 10:27).

God not only told *us* to love, but also sent Jesus to show how much *He* loves us. God's laws were simply schoolmasters put in place to lead us toward Jesus (Galatians 3:24). When we receive

Jesus, when His Holy Spirit lives within us, love, joy, peace, patience, kindness, goodness, faithfulness, gentleness, and self-control become not laws, but fruits (Galatians 5:22, 23). In any situation, we rely on the Spirit. Instead of asking, "What is the rule?" we ask, "What does LOVE do? What does God's Spirit say? What fruit is operative here?"

Our Discipline

When we discipline children, we go by God's Kingdom Principles:

1. LOVE comes first.

2. SEPARATION is the result of wrong choices.

3. SHOW THE WAY.

Discipline is guiding children toward certain behavior choices. At first, the guidance is external. But our rules are designed to cultivate in children a heart that grows the fruits of the Spirit, one of which is self-control. Our goal is to bring children to the place where they are self-controlled. When we looked at the moral development of children, we saw that this is an ongoing process. (If you are like me, you are still in process.)

Discipline, or discipling, is a two-sided coin. One side is direction and the other is correction. A ship captain directs his ship toward its destination. So we direct a child toward his destination: self-control. But if the ship gets off course and goes the wrong direction, the captain must make a course correction to get it back on the right course. So a child must correct his course if he has gone the wrong direction. Children often need help with course corrections. That's where we come in.

Direction

Believe it or not, everything you have read so far in this book has to do with discipline. That's because it all has to do with setting a positive direction for your child or your class. Positive direction helps prevent the need for correction.

Guidance

Direction 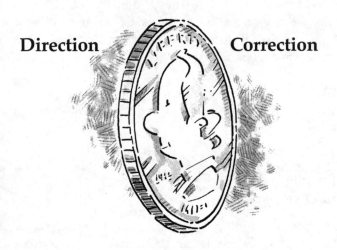 Correction

Let's review some of the factors that keep us headed in the right direction:

1. Stop, look and listen.
   Observe the children in your class. Listen to them.

2. Build a relationship with the children.
   A good relationship helps build trust. According to pediatrician William Sears, "Respect for authority is based on trust."[1]

3. Know what age-appropriate behavior to expect from your children.
   Review the chapters on development as often as you need to.

4. Communicate in ways that your children will understand.

5. Have a plan, and then take **AIM**:
   Make lessons **Age-Appropriate**, **Interesting**, and **Meaningful**.

6. Be flexible and make variety the key when choosing activities.

7. Make variety and believability your goal for telling Bible stories.

8. Be excited about your class.
   If you're not excited, then change what you can, in order to get excited.

Let's look at some other specifics in the area of direction and prevention. Grace Mitchell in her book *A Very Practical Guide to Discipline with Young Children* suggests that we anticipate behavior problems by looking at possible triggers in three areas: people, environment, and program.[2] We can do a check-up by asking ourselves some questions about each of these areas.

1. People: Teacher, Children and Parents

Do we, as teachers, arrive early for class? When the teacher is there before the children arrive, the teacher sets the tone for what will happen in the classroom. The children enter the teacher's territory, and the teacher is in charge. But if the children arrive before the teacher does, the children set the tone for what will happen. The teacher enters the children's territory. Who's in charge then?

Are we prepared? It's hard for us to greet children when we're running around looking for the red construction paper and scissors, or punching out the handwork for the day. Some children misbehave to get attention, and the busy-with-materials teacher creates a situation that invites this child to misbehave.

Do we pray for the children during the week? We can post a list of our children's names at home where we'll be reminded to pray for them and their families. While we're greeting children and visiting with them before class, we can say a silent, short prayer for each one. No one even needs to be aware of what we're doing. We can do this during class activities, too.

Do we love the children? Dr. Slonecker, a respected pediatrician says, "Tell the child every class time, 'I love you.' If he understands you love him, you'll be able to discipline him better."[3] That's because when children feel loved by someone, they want to please that person. "Every child really wants… approval of a favorite adult," writes Grace Mitchell.[4]

Do certain children always misbehave when they're around each other? If you can, separate the children who tempt each other to misbehave. Sometimes this means placing two friends at opposite sides of the story rug, because they are so friendly, they whisper and giggle when it's time to listen. Or it may involve two rough and tumble little boys (or girls) who itch to wrestle every time they're near each other. It's not that these children are intentionally trying to disrupt the class. They are following their natural instincts to have a good time with good friends. Anticipate this, and separate the children into different groups or areas if you can.

Do we tell children when they have choices and when they don't? If you don't want the child to choose, don't give him a choice. For example, let's say you want the children to put the blocks away and gather on the rug for story time. Avoid asking, "Would you like to come hear a story now?" Someone will answer, "No." You have given them a choice. Instead, say, "It's time to put the blocks away and come to the rug for a story."

Do we give advance warning when activities are going to change? You don't like someone to come up to you when you are busy and say, "Come on, let's go! Right now!" If you can give advance notice, then do. It's always good to let kids know before a change of activities. For example, "In five minutes, we'll put the blocks away and gather at the story rug."

Are we specific? If we say, "Put that over there," the child may put something else somewhere else, because we weren't specific. Later, we see "that" was not put over "there," and we think the child has not obeyed. If only we had been specific, the child would have known that we meant for him to put the toy truck on the bottom shelf.

Have we communicated the rules to the children? We can't expect children to keep the rules if they don't know what the rules are.

Are parents treated with respect? Are they kept informed about what is happening in the classroom? Are they consulted when you have a problem or question about a child?

2. Environment

Is your room too large or too open? When I taught four-year-olds, we were in a small classroom. I would often look longingly down the hall at the nice big room the kindergartners used. I would think, "Wouldn't it be nice to have a spacious classroom like that?" Then one year, my class moved to that big room. But I was puzzled. This group of kids was different than last year's class. When these kids came into the classroom, they immediately began racing back and forth. It was hard to settle them down.

Then I began to look at the environment, and I realized what had happened. This year's kids weren't any different than last year's. What was different was the room. I began to look at it from a child's perspective. It was like a gymnasium to them, and it invited running. The solution to my problem was easy. I blocked the "raceway." I moved a table and chairs into the open space. I rearranged the bookshelf, easels, sand table, and other furniture so the temptation to run was no longer a factor. My class was much more self-controlled.

Is the room too crowded? If a child has to walk through the book center to get to the blocks, the children who are peacefully looking at books will be disturbed. They'll get frustrated. Then they'll be tempted to trip or hit children who pass through. Some children who are crowded do what their instincts tell them to do:

they push. It's their way of communicating. They are saying, "Give me more space. You're crowding me."

Is the room age-appropriate? Are tables and chairs the right size? Are there colorful pictures on the walls? Is the setting informal so it welcomes all kinds of learners?

Is the room neat, but not sterile? A messy room will tell the children that the teacher doesn't care, so they won't care if they mess it up even more. But a room that's too neat is not inviting or comfortable. It makes kids feel like they can't do anything for fear of messing something up.

3. Program

Does your schedule fit the needs of the children? Are they getting restless just when you've tried to settle them down for group time? Maybe you should change the time for your large group activity. Could they be hungry? Do you need to schedule a snack at this time? Is it time for something active? Is it time for a rest?

When do problems occur? Do they happen when you change from one activity to another? If so, you may need to think of ways to make the transition smoother. Could you make a "path" of masking tape the children follow from one center to another? Could you sing or play a tape while they change groups?

Do you have a plan for getting everyone's attention? Equip your classroom with some type of signal to use when you want to get the students' attention. I use a bell. When I ring the bell, everyone is supposed to sit down where they are, "freeze," look at me, and listen. We even play this as a game in order to practice the procedure. Other teachers flick overhead lights off when everyone is to get quiet. Some teachers sing a simple song, and the children can join in.

Do you have enough activities? Do you have things planned for those kids who finish an activity quickly? Do you have enough variety in the activities you've chosen? Change the games, puzzles, and toys in the room from time to time to keep it interesting. Is class time fun? Are the activities enjoyable? Do you make choices available? Are you excited yourself? If you're not excited to come to class, the children will not be excited either.

Do you give the children tasks they can achieve? Do they feel successful in class?

Are you consistent? If co-teachers and aides have different expectations, there will be problems. Changing your rules or your enforcement of the rules from week to week will cause problems too.

After the children know what is expected of them, they will often test you to see if the boundaries are going to hold. Don and Jeanne Elium, authors of *Raising a Son*, write that children want to know "Who's the boss... what are the rules... and are you going to enforce them?"[5] Consistent enforcement of the boundaries makes children feel secure. The teacher can be counted on to keep the classroom a safe and welcoming place.

It's a good idea to ask the children to help make the rules. Then they feel like this is indeed their classroom. They see themselves as valued decision makers. If the children make the rules, they are quicker to abide by them and to see that others in class do too. However, they may be more strict in making their rules than you are, and you might want to soften their intensity.

Try to have only a few rules, and state them positively. For older children, write the rules on a chart and post it in your classroom. For younger children, you might use pictures as symbols to represent each rule. In my four-year-old class, we had four rules, written on a poster in "rebus" form: We are "happy" (designated with a smiley face) to "help" (shown by a handprint). We are "happy" (smiley face) to "share" (a hand holding an apple). We are "happy" (smiley face) to "love" (shown by a heart). We are "happy" (smiley face) to "obey" (shown by a big letter O). We "read" these sentences at the beginning of each group time for several weeks until I feel sure the children will remember them. We can read them to review any time we need to, and we can talk about specific actions that show "love" and "obedience."

Now What?

There's an old fable about three blind men who were walking down a road one day, traveling to a world famous bazaar. There they would smell the wonderful spices and feel the rolls of silks. They would hear the music of pipers and buy sweet, cool fruit juices.

The blind men had not gone far when they came to an elephant standing in the middle of the road. The first blind man bumped into the elephant's trunk. When he felt it, he declared that they had stumbled across a snake. He concluded that they must have come upon a snakes' den. They would have to circle around until they were sure they had avoided the snakes. Then they could go on their way.

But the second blind man was feeling the elephant's tall, wide side. He insisted that they had bumped into a wall. They would definitely have to climb over it.

The third blind man had his arms around one of the elephant's legs. He announced that he had run into a tree. He decided they must be entering a dense jungle. They would need to make their way slowly and carefully through the trees.

The blind men began to argue. None of them could agree on what they had bumped into or how they should proceed. Finally, because they could not agree, they just turned around and went back home.

That's sometimes the way it is with the question of discipline. We are going along our merry way, doing all we can to prevent misbehavior, when we bump into a child whose behavior challenges us. "What's this?" we ask. We're not sure why the child is misbehaving. We're not sure what to do about it. We know we need to help the child make a course correction, but the area of correction is like the elephant. Different experts look at it and give different opinions. What do we do? The next chapter gives specific suggestions regarding why children misbehave and what to do about it.

Chapter 17

On the Other Side of the Coin

Correcting Behavior

"Never give up.
Keep on trying until you get it right."
- 5 year old

Seeing Our Opportunity

In the face of challenges, my father often says, "You can see it as a problem, or you can see it as an opportunity." If we look at behavior challenges as opportunities instead of problems, we have a better chance of bringing about positive change. Misbehavior is our opportunity to do what we're here to do: teach. Here is a real-life chance to help a child learn how to handle his problems, to help a child get her needs met. If we take the challenge of this opportunity, we can affect the child's life, his future choices, her understanding of how to relate to God and others. Instead of simply trying to squelch negative behavior so we can get through our material or make it until the bell signals the end of class time, we work with children to help them understand that certain behaviors don't work. We show them a better way.

So when children misbehave, our first assumption should be:

1) They don't know how to solve their problems or get their needs met.

There are two other possibilities:

2) They don't immediately remember the correct behavior.

3) They don't trust that the right behavior will work, so they go against what they've been taught.

Reasons for a Child's Challenging Behavior

In order to teach children how to solve problems and make the right behavior choices, we need to think about what might be at the root of the misbehavior. Understanding the child's misbehavior does not mean you condone it. It simply means that you are more able to accurately deal with the behavior with a loving response as you set and maintain limits.

Here are the most common causes of misbehavior.

1. Physical Needs

The younger the child is, the more his physical condition affects his behavior. But even with older children, when misbehavior occurs, the first cause to consider is the physical. Illness, allergies, sleepiness, hunger, being too hot or too cold, and even sitting still too long can be factors that could be at the root of a child's misbehavior.

What do you do? Once you suspect that a physical factor is the root of the problem, you meet the physical need the best you can. Provide snacks if you think children are hungry. Contact parents if you suspect illness or allergy. I've been in more than one class in which we provided a soft, out-of-the-way place for a sleepy child to nap.

If you can provide for physical needs, misbehavior due to this need will probably disappear. However, if necessary, you can allow consequences to be the teacher. You will find these in the next section of this chapter.

2. Environmental or Scheduling Factors

Perhaps the child does not know the rules. Or the teacher is late or preoccupied. Maybe the child finds the class boring. Or the classroom or furniture may be too large or too small. Activities and toys may not be age-appropriate. Or the children may need an active break in order to stretch and move for awhile.

What do you do? Environmental and scheduling factors were covered in greater depth in the previous chapter about preventing misbehavior. If you suspect that the problem might lie in factors which are under your control, try changing the schedule or the environment and see if that will take care of the problem.

As a reminder: Understanding the child's misbehavior does not mean you condone it. It simply means that you are more able to accurately deal with the behavior with a loving response as you set and maintain limits. If you can provide for environmental and scheduling needs, misbehavior due to these factors will probably disappear. However, if necessary, you can allow consequences to be the teacher. You will find these in the next section of this chapter.

3. Need for Loving Attention

Dr. Ross Campbell says, "The main cause of misbehavior is an empty emotional tank."[1] Unfortunately, when a child needs loving attention and can't get it, she'll settle for any kind of attention. That's why this child may come to class and exhibit behavior that annoys you. According to L. Tobin, your annoyed feeling is the signal that this child's need is attention.[2]

What do you do? Ignore the annoying behavior if you can. Then be sure to give the child loving attention at other times. You may need to meet with co-teachers and decide that one of you will make this child a priority in the attention department. Also, be aware of the fact that the first five minutes of class time are very important for this child. So make sure someone is meeting and greeting the children, and pay special attention to this attention-starved child when he or she arrives.

As a reminder: Understanding the child's misbehavior does not mean you condone it. It simply means that you are more able to accurately deal with the behavior with a loving response as you set and maintain limits. If you can provide for attention needs, misbehavior due to this factor will probably disappear. However, if necessary, you can allow consequences to be the teacher. You will find these in the next section of this chapter.

4. Need for Leadership Opportunity

God has given us lots of children who are potential leaders. And leaders want to lead. They want power. They may not want to be under authority. How does this make you feel? It probably makes you feel angry, because you are the leader and you are trying to lead, but this child does not want to follow. L. Tobin says that your anger is the signal that this child wants power.

What do you do? First of all, try to detach yourself. That means don't take it personally. If you are angry, or if the child is angry, give yourselves time to cool off before discussing it. When you talk, in order to avoid a power play between you and the child, focus on the rules of your classroom. This is one time you'll be glad you communicated the rules in a way the children can understand. Posting the rules in the classroom will also help. Now you refer to those rules, asking the child to repeat the one that is applicable to this situation. Be calm and cheerful, but firm. Affirm to the child that she is a leader, and tell her that this is why you can't let her get away with misbehavior. Tell her that a good leader must first learn to obey, to be under authority.

You will also need to give leaders the leadership opportunities they need. Ask these children to lead songs or hand out materials or read the scripture. Find other responsibilities they can take in the classroom. For younger children, allowing them to make choices will help them feel like they have more autonomy in the situation. For example, instead of getting into a power play over whether the child will hold your hand or not, ask the child, "Which hand do you want me to hold: this one or that one?"

As a reminder: Understanding the child's misbehavior does not mean you condone it. It simply means that you are more able to accurately deal with the behavior with a loving response as you set and maintain limits. If oppositional behavior continues, however, you may find it necessary to let consequences be the teacher. You will find these in the next section of this chapter.

5. Need for Relational Skills

I want to play, but I don't know how to ask. So I poke or punch or pinch.

Someone just grabbed the marker I was using or the toy I was playing with. I don't know what to do, so I kick.

I want the glue and another boy has it. Or I want the toy another girl is playing with. I don't know how to get it. So I grab it.

I've been reading quietly, but these other kids keep playing loudly right next to me. They're tripping over me. I don't know what to do. So I hit them.

In all these instances, children lack the relational skills to get their needs met. How do you know? Someone or something ends up getting hurt, either emotionally or physically. If you need the child to tell you about the situation, say, "Tell me what happened." If you ask, "Why did you do that?" you probably won't get the information you need. Children don't usually know why they did it. Asking why also makes it easy for children to blame someone else.

What do you do? If the hurting is currently in process (as with a fight, for example), you must move in and separate the children immediately. Your job is to keep the children safe. Then you go to the victim first and give attention to that child's needs. You also teach this child how to respond when treated that way. Then you talk to the aggressor. Stay calm, but be firm.

Dr. Becky Bailey gives us a helpful procedure to follow when teaching these kinds of relational skills.[3]

Teach the victim to speak up, by simply saying, "Don't" or "No" or "I don't like it when you _____."

For the aggressor, say:
<u>Motive</u>: You wanted _____, so you _____.
<u>Need</u>: You didn't know the words to say (or what else to do).
<u>Limit</u>: You may not_____. _____-ing hurts.
<u>Teach</u>: When you want _____, say (or do) _____.

You may also want the child to practice saying or doing what you suggest.

When you follow this procedure or something like this, you are teaching valuable skills that the child can use the rest of his life. Now you are not only teaching a Bible story from which you extract the moral of the story: Be kind. You are also modeling kindness yourself as you handle this situation. And you are teaching children how to apply kindness to their real life needs.

Some people may question telling a child, "You didn't know the words to say (or what else to do)." Are we excusing the child? Didn't he know better than to do that? If he did know, he forgot, or he thought it wouldn't work in this situation. Actually when we say, "You didn't know what you were doing," we are echoing Jesus' words when He said, "Father, forgive them, for they do not know what they are doing" (Luke 23:34).

As a reminder, understanding the child's misbehavior does not mean you condone it. It simply means that you are more able to accurately deal with the behavior with a loving response as you set and maintain limits. If a child continues to have difficulty remembering the way to handle these relational situations, you may find it necessary to let consequences be the teacher. You will find these in the next section of this chapter.

6. Frustration

A boy seems to be content working a puzzle. You are helping another child when the puzzle pieces go flying past and scatter across the floor. You wonder what in the world happened.

A girl has slipped her tie-shoes off and is now trying to get them back on so she can join an activity. The faster she works at the knots, the longer it takes her. The activity is starting without her. In a minute a shoe slams against the wall. You wonder what's going on.

Your feelings of puzzlement or despair are a sign that this behavior is rooted in frustration or, according to L. Tobin, a feeling of inadequacy. You yourself often end up frustrated by the behavior. What do you do? Stay calm. Be cheerful, but firm. Follow the steps outlined in section 5 above, stating the motive, need, limit, and teaching.

There's another kind of frustration that we should deal with differently: the tantrum. A tantrum is frustration at not being able to control a situation. Things aren't going the way the child wants them to go. Most often, we think of tantrums as being physical. But tantrums can be verbal, too. A child yelling at you or another child is having a verbal tantrum.

What do you do? First, remain calm. Keep your cool. It won't help to have two tantrums going on, one from the child and one from you. Be cheerful but firm. However, it doesn't work to try to reason with someone who is flailing around or yelling. The most we can do at this point is try to help the tantrum subside by empathizing with the upset child. Paul tells us to "mourn with those who mourn" (Romans 12:15). Hebrews tells us that Jesus is able to sympathize with our weaknesses, having been tempted in the same ways we're tempted. Have you been tempted, even as an adult, to throw a verbal or physical tantrum? Then you can sympathize. You can empathize.

Dr. Bailey gives us some pointers to remember when dealing with tantrums: Reflect what you **see** and **hear** and what you sense the child **feels**. ("I see your arms flying and your feet kicking. I hear you yelling. I think you feel angry.") Allow the tantrum to subside. Then go through the steps outlined above so that you can teach: motive, need, limit, and teaching.

Sometimes you can redirect the child. This works especially well with younger children, and is used almost exclusively for children younger than 18 months old. Distract their attention to something else. Show them what else they might do. Physically move them if you need to.

If the tantrum is physically hurting the child or someone else, you will have to restrain the child. Dr. Bailey suggests holding the child until she calms down. You'll need to tell the child that it's your job to keep everyone safe and you won't let her hurt anyone, nor will you let anyone hurt her.

As a reminder, understanding the child's misbehavior does not mean you condone it. It simply means that you are more able to accurately deal with the behavior with a loving response as you set and maintain limits. If a child continues to have difficulty remembering the way to handle frustration, you may find it necessary to let consequences be the teacher.

Consequences

Hemfelt and Warren write, "Actions invite consequences. By giving a child a choice of actions, each with its attendant consequences, we can reinforce the cardinal rule: What happens to you is up to you."[4] If you have tried to teach a child the best you can but the challenging behavior persists, you may need to allow the child to experience the consequences of his continuing misbehavior. This, too, is part of discipline (discipling and training).

1. Natural Consequences

This type of consequence is called "natural," because it occurs without your involvement. For example, four-year-old James brings a small truck to class. He has it in his pocket for awhile, but then he pulls it out and shows it to the other children. You tell James to keep the truck in his pocket so it won't get lost. But James doesn't obey you. So you let the natural consequence happen. After class, James returns to your room with his mother, looking for his truck. At this point you don't say, "I told you so." James has learned his lesson. So you sympathize and help him think: "You've lost your toy truck? I'll help you look for it. What could you do next time to keep it from getting lost?"

2. Imposed Consequences

These are consequences you create. They should be logically related to the behavior.

- *Remove the material.* If Brittany keeps squirting her glue onto her neighbor's paper, remove the glue.

- *Remove the privilege.* If Megan continues to leave her mess on the table after every craft activity, she loses the privilege of doing the craft. A couple of notes here: 1) If it's not a privilege, removing it won't be effective. 2) Be sure you don't remove a privilege that the child needs in order to help his behavior. Teachers used to make misbehaving children stay in the classroom during recess. But recess is exactly what these children needed in order to run off the steam that aggravated the misbehavior in the first place. Or another example: Taking snack privileges away from a child who needs a snack only makes the situation worse.

- *Remove the child from the situation.* If Andrew continues to wrestle with children who are trying to watch a DVD, Andrew is removed from the group. We sometimes call this "time out." It was originally called "time out from positive reinforcement," which means the child gets no attention during time out. If the child gets up, physically take him back to the chair. Start timing all over again. If he is loud, he has to sit until he is quiet, then the timing starts again.

If you choose time-out, use a timer instead of counting on yourself to keep up with the time. A good way to decide how long to leave a child in time-out is to think of his age. Usually a child can handle as many minutes as his age in years. A five-year-old can handle five minutes. A four year old can take four minutes, and so on. Time-out can be started at about 18 months. At that age, an assistant in class may have to hold the child gently but firmly without talking.

If you are working with a child who gets "revved up," and if you are able to communicate with him about the feelings he has when he starts to get out of control, you can make a quiet, alone space available to him. This would be a place where he can go to be by himself to calm down. He can learn to choose this time-out himself when he feels like he's starting to lose control, or you can agree on a secret symbol (like fingers crossed or thumbs up) that you will give him to suggest that he calm down or retreat to his quiet spot if necessary.

Long-Term Training

Occasionally you will need to work with a particular child over an extended period of time to help him choose the right behavior. Richard Lavoie points out that success is the only true motivator.[5] We are trying to give children that glowing and powerful sense of success that comes with being able to control their own behavior. Here are some ways to remind children of what they've been taught and to motivate them to choose the right behavior.

Counting Down

For younger children, counting "1, 2, 3," after telling them what to do gives them time to choose to comply. Pause a second or two after each number. If you are working with a child on a particular behavior, you might even be able to start counting without saying anything else. "John, 1, 2, 3." He will know that you've seen him struggling to make the right choice, and you're giving him a chance to control himself.

Secret Signal

This is related to counting down, but it's a signal you've agreed on with the child in private. It's between you and him. When he sees you make the signal (pulling on one of your ears, crossing your fingers, even a thumbs up), it's his reminder to control her behavior.

A Sense of Humor

Sometimes responding humorously will defuse the situation and get the desired behavior. For example, young children sometimes say, "No," just to make the statement that they are becoming independent. I try at first to smile, reach down, and tickle them gently. In a playful tone, I say, "No? What do you mean no?" Then I repeat the instructions, and often the child complies.

Or you can tell a child, "Throw your grumpies (or loud voice or wigglies or grabbies or wrestles) outside. They can wait for you there, and you can get them again when you go back out the door." Then you can pretend to throw the grumpies out. If the child is young, you can even walk with him to the door, pretend to put the grumpies by the door and say, "Stay there!"

Again, these are ways to give the child a reminder and the time to make a better behavior decision for himself.

Charts and Rewards

Reward charts can be an indicator of success *if that's what a child needs and responds to.* Remember that we are talking about using these as long-term training in specific areas. Some children need a visual reminder of their achievement in controlling their behavior. Make the chart simple and fun. You can place stickers on a chart for good behavior. Or draw smiley faces next to the child's name.

For maximum effect, I think the chart should be private, between you and the child you are working with. This is part of building a relationship with the child and tells him you are on his side, wanting to help him learn to help himself. It tells him you believe he can and will achieve. So you will meet with him briefly and tell him you want to work with him to, for example, help him keep his hands to himself in class. Explain why. You might explain that hitting hurts other people, and one of your jobs is to make sure everyone is safe. Or hitting starts fights and causes other people to have a hard time controlling themselves. Or other children don't want to play with someone who hits them, etc. Then show the child the chart. Work out a signal as discussed above. Toward the end of class time, briefly get together with the child and encourage him by telling him you see he's working hard (or thinking hard) about choosing the right behavior. As he achieves your goal, mark it on the chart.

This brings us to the subject of rewards for good behavior. Some people refuse to give rewards, because they feel that rewards are bribes. But a bribe is payment that someone receives in return for going against his conscience. Rewards are not bribes; rewards indicate achievement. However, it is important to note:

- Some children are *not* motivated by rewards.
- Rewards should be given for a specific, agreed-upon behavior.
- If rewards are the only behavior incentive, given for everything you want the child to do, then rewards lose their effectiveness.
- The younger the child, the shorter time there should be between the proper behavior and the reward, or between the misbehavior and the consequence. If a three-year-old has to wait four weeks for his reward, he will soon give up.

Think of rewards in the sense of earning a scout badge. The badge is a sign that says something was achieved by hard work. Since we're looking at rewards in terms of long-term training, we should remember that some children have to work very hard to control themselves. If you have worked out a plan ahead of time with the child, and he is working to achieve an entire class time without hitting another child, for example, you may want to reward his hard work. Your smile and encouraging words may be all that are needed. On the other hand, you might add a sticker or a hand stamp.

For longer term, especially at home where there is more time to work on the desired behavior, earning coupons, pizza points, ice cream points, pennies collected in a jar, or miscellaneous prizes may be effective. Remember, though: The greatest reward is the feeling of success the child experiences through 1) her own achievement (even small successes) in controlling herself and 2) your encouragement as you recognize her hard work. The pizza, ice cream, or pennies are a celebration of her hard work and should be accompanied by your expressions of gratitude.

Connect the Dots Chart

Decide what the reward will be: ice cream coupon, fast food coupon, a pair of sunglasses. Draw that item in dot-to-dot form. The child can connect the dots, moving ahead one dot for each class time that has been completed with acceptable behavior. As soon as the child completes her dot-to-dot, you celebrate by giving her the prize she's earned. This is a one-time process. The child may slip once in awhile and return to the challenging behavior, but don't go back to the chart. Simply continue to let her know you have confidence she'll make the right choice next time. If the challenging behavior becomes a habit again, you may need to try a different path of training.

Pocket Cards

This is a visual reminder. Get one small envelope for each child. Cut the flaps off the envelopes and glue the fronts of the envelopes to a poster board. Write one child's name on each envelope. Place three colored index cards in each envelope: green, yellow, and red in that order with the green at the front.

The colors of the cards correspond to a traffic light. When the green is showing, it means the child is remembering to make the right choices. But if the child misbehaves, he must pull out the green card and place it behind the other cards to reveal the yellow card. The yellow means "warning." If he has to put the yellow card at the back, the red card is revealed. That means he has chosen the negative consequence you've discussed with him.

Teachers who have used this system say it works well. Rarely do their students get past the warning stage.

Pocket Cards

Other Ideas

Having class "meetings" for a few minutes once a month will help keep everyone aware of the rules. Let the kids tell you if they are having any problems. Let them help you decide if rules need to be changed. If there are behavior problems, the children themselves can suggest solutions.

You should feel free to discuss behavior problems with the child's parents. Parents are usually glad to be consulted. Approach the situation as a friend of both parent and child. Don't tell parents what a bad child they have. Instead, tell them you're learning how to work with their child, and ask them if they have found a method that is effective at home and might work in the classroom as well. If the child is hyperactive or learning disabled or has another physical or emotional reason for behaving the way he does, the parent is probably your best source of information about how to work with him.

As God Does

We started our discussion about behavior by discovering God's Kingdom Principles: 1) Love, 2) Separation, and 3) Showing the way. Let's briefly revisit those principles.

1) Love

What does God say about misbehaving? "When people sin, you should forgive and comfort them, so they won't give up in despair. You should make them sure of your love for them" (II Corinthians 2:7, CEV). "Do as God does. . . . Let love be your guide" (Ephesians 5:1).

2) Separation

It's interesting to note that the imposed consequences listed above are all different forms of separation: separating the child from material, separating him from privilege, separating him from the situation. God used these forms of separation Himself. He separated Adam and Eve from their privilege of living in the Garden of Eden. When the Israelites collected more manna than God told them to gather, the extra manna spoiled, effectively separating them from the material. Jonah spent three days and nights in Time Out in the belly of a huge fish. The Israelites spent 40 years of Time Out in the wilderness. They forfeited their privilege of going into the Promised Land. They were separated from the new situation God wanted them to experience.

3) Show the Way

It's easy to focus on what children do wrong and overlook what they do right. But God doesn't just point out wrong, He shows what's right. He gives us a vision for who we are. He encourages us. So we need to watch for good behaviors and reinforce them with encouragement. "You shared!" "You were very persistent on your project! Well done!" "You put the trash in the trash can without even being asked! You are so thoughtful!"

A Tale to Remember

There's a tale that's told about the sun and wind. The wind boasted, "I'm stronger than you." But the sun said, "No, I'm stronger than you."

The wind and sun argued back and forth for some time, until they saw a traveler coming over the hill. The wind said, "I'll prove I'm stronger. I will blow that traveler's coat off." So the wind began to blow.

However, the more the wind blew, the closer the traveler pulled his coat around him. At last the wind blew himself out.

"It's my turn," said the sun. He began to shine.

The traveler, no longer cold, loosened his coat. With every step, he grew warmer and warmer. Finally he was so hot, he took his coat off.

The moral of the story is: When it comes to discipline, you can get more done by shining than you can by blowing.

The Growing
TEACHER

Chapter 18

What About Me?

Needs of the Teacher

"We constantly search for ways that we can 'change the child.'
Perhaps the first significant change
should come from us."
- Richard Lavoie [1]

The Mission

You open a little black box and push a button inside. A tape begins to play. "Your mission, should you decide to accept it…" The impossibly difficult mission is described. Then the tape self-destructs. After all the information is given, the important question remains: Should you decide to accept it?

I want to be totally honest with you here. Earlier, I mentioned the statistics: 80% to 90% of our kids are now leaving the church after graduating from high school. I have been involved in Christian education since I was 14 years old. That's over forty years. As I look back over the past 15 years (the time in which the kids now leaving church were in our Christian ed programs), here's what I see. We have done our best with the latest in music, puppets, storytelling, learning centers, child safety, etc. We now have majors in children's ministry at many of our Christian colleges and universities, so we are graduating people who have expressed a desire to work with children, teachers, and parents. But there is one thing that has been a problem for years, one thing that creeps into church educators' conversations at every conference, one thing that continues to plague us. We cannot get teachers who will commit long-term.

We can hardly get teachers to commit short-term. One educator remarked that adults are not willing to pay the price. What's the price? Time. Time to do the hard work. Time to build relationship with children. Time away from adult assemblies, from the care and feeding of ourselves.

This same educator pointed out that young people leaving the church are voting with their feet. They are telling us, "I sang your songs. I jumped to your music. I ate your pizza. But I did not meet your God." I go into great detail on this in *I Want to Believe But I Can't*, so I won't rehash it here. Suffice it to say for our purposes in this book: Here's the mission. Should you decide to accept it Can you commit to it? Can you be the teacher of the four-year-olds or the second-graders for an entire nine months or a year? Because that's what they need, someone to care enough about them to get to know them, to be there for them, to build relationship with them, to be "*my teacher*."

The truth is, being a teacher is hard work.

Commentator David Kupelian says, "In past eras, if parents were very imperfect or even corrupt, their children still had a reasonable chance of 'growing up straight,' since the rest of society still more or less reflected Judeo-Christian values. The youngster could bond to a teacher, minister, mentor or organization that could provide some healthy direction and stability."[2] Have we abandoned our kids by refusing to take the time and make the effort to build relationships with them?

The truth is, being a teacher is hard work. As with anything you dedicate yourself to, there are ups and downs. There are times when you feel like no one appreciates all the hard work you're doing. But the ultimate rewards for your dedication and persistence will go far beyond what you could ever imagine. I'm not just talking about heaven. When a young man volunteers to be a new teacher in a preschool classroom, and you realize he was a boy you taught when he was four, that's a priceless reward. I know.

Now, I have a theory about one reason it's hard to recruit and keep teachers. Yes, definitely time is a factor, stress is another, self-care is another. But lack of training is a factor too. This applies to those of you who are supervisors or are planning to take on such positions. It may also apply to you as a teacher, if your church is not training you and your fellow-teachers. For many years in many churches, the modus operandi was to get volunteers for each class, meet one Saturday to hand out the lesson plans and give a general meet-your-co-teacher and here's-the-schedule talk, then send the troops in. At the end of a few weeks, teachers emerged from their classrooms battered and weary and under-appreciated, many of them vowing never to return. They shared their negative experiences with friends, who vowed never to volunteer and subject themselves to a situation like that.

Of course, if you've gotten this far in this book, you've had some book-training at least. I hope you will take it into the classroom. I hope you will be persistent and determined and dedicated and child-sensitive. If you listen to children, and if you are willing to be flexible and adjust to their needs and interests, you will find that *they* will teach you how to teach. God gave us children to grow us up.

Your Own Stages

Erikson's stages of development continue through adulthood.[3] The stage of developing our identity, the task we focused on with adolescence, actually is not completed until the early 20's. Then we go through a period of **transition** in which our task is to develop either **intimacy** or **isolation.** Intimacy develops from having a friend who can know everything about us, yet never waver in his or her friendship. Out of this sense of intimacy grows the strength of love. At this stage, a growing faith revolves in cycles of reflection and recommitment. We reflect on our beliefs, perhaps question them, seek more, and then recommit.[4] I think of it as journeying up a mountain on a path that goes around and around, always upward, headed toward the top.

Our 30's through 60's take us through a new stage in which our task is to develop **generativity.** Failing that, we go through **stagnation.** Generativity means high productivity, generating goods, services, and ideas for the marketplace, growing relationships, taking our place in the ever-churning world and producing for our fellow-humans. Generativity also has to do with generations. Part of the reason we produce and generate and grow has to do with providing for the next generation. Erikson says that when we achieve generativity, as opposed to stagnation, the strength that develops is **care**. Faith at this stage is usually less idealistic. It includes accepting hardships as a reality of life as we continue to cycle between reflecting and recommitting.

The next stage is **Older Adulthood**. According to Erikson, during this stage we develop either a sense of **integrity** or a sense of **despair**. Integrity comes when we are satisfied with the fullness of life. Despair comes with regrets and loss of hope. Faith now includes deeper understandings that come from our own experiences as we have walked with God. If we are living in the positive, the sense of integrity, the strength that develops in this stage is **wisdom**. And faith? If it's still growing (and it should be), we still cycle between reflecting and recommitting.

So I hope you are discontent with where you are spiritually. I hope you are on the journey around the mountain, reflecting and recommitting. There is no retirement. "The righteous will flourish like a palm tree, they will grow like a cedar of Lebanon... They will still bear fruit in old age, they will stay fresh and green, proclaiming, 'The Lord is upright; he is my Rock, and there is no wickedness in him'" (Psalm 92:12-15).

What's Your Why?

When we surveyed the developmental stages of childhood, I often mentioned "taken-for-granted faith," which is believing something is true simply because you were told it's true. I pointed out that one option in adolescence is to hang on to taken-for-granted faith and never personalize it. A lot of us did that in the past, and we got away with it, because it looked like personalized faith. Instead, it was a personalized assent to a set of doctrines and beliefs. But if asked why we believed in Jesus, many of us simply scrolled back in our memories to pull out the reasons given us by someone else.

If you can't explain why you believe, I *don't* think that means you're not saved. Since faith development is a process, not an event, and since we must "grow up into our salvation," I think anytime we commit – or recommit – ourselves to Jesus, we acknowledge Him as the Way and identify our lives with Him and His purposes. So what I'm talking about when I speak of the "why" is being able to tell others, in this case children and youth, the reason you are a Christian. It no longer convinces young people in our postmodern culture to say, "You just have to have faith." Or to say in our pluralistic culture, "I believe because the Bible says..." Every religion has their scriptures and sacred writings. Every religion has their handed-down teachings. Kids want to know why Christianity is your religion of choice, and why Jesus is the Way and not Buddhism or Islam or agnosticism.[5]

A glib, canned reason does not help kids talk about Christianity and faith in Jesus among their classmates and friends. If Jesus is the Way, then there's a reason He's the Way. If He's the Truth and kids know why, then they don't have to be afraid or overwhelmed in a discussion about Buddhism and Islam.

Believe it or not, I spoke at a recent gathering of teachers who had no idea that their city had two Buddhist temples and a mosque. Have we been blind to the struggles our kids are having (or will have) in our global, pluralistic, postmodern culture? Have we preferred to keep our heads in the sand and simply teach the material on Sunday morning, thinking that's sufficient? Of course we need "the material," the curricula. But the curricula is secondary. Kids are our priority. We are in the classroom to teach *kids*. But when we teach kids, we need to grapple with the issues they struggle with. We need to listen to their questions. We need to join their conversation. We need to dig for answers.

That brings us back to the "why." One of kids' questions is, or should be, "Why be a Christian?" We have taught kids "what": the facts about the Bible and life as a Christian. We have taught them "how": how to pray, how to memorize scriptures, how to become a Christian, and how to live the Christian life. But have we skipped the why? Why does it make sense to choose Christianity? Do I believe in Jesus just so I can stay out of hell?

Other religions have their versions of hell too, and they have their own ways of staying out. What makes Jesus the Way?

I spoke about the "why" to teachers at a conference not too long ago. I asked them how they, as teachers, explain to kids why they themselves believe. One teacher raised his hand and said he tells kids to look at the stars. He said he doesn't see how anyone can *not* believe if they simply look at the heavens. That's fine for him personally. If that's why he believes, then I can't deny *his* belief *for him*. But does that "why" work for children or youth? Does it work with his neighbor? Plenty of atheists look at the stars and never believe in Jesus. Even if you look at the stars and say to yourself, *There has to be a God*, do the stars show that there is one and only one God? Do they prove He sent His Son? All I'm trying to say is that you owe it to your students to wrestle with these things and come up with a reason that is reasonable to *them*.

If you want to explore these issues further with me, you might want to read *Love Trumps Karma* and/or *Mall of Religions* as well as *I Want to Believe But I Can't*. In this last book, I talk about other questions kids ask, such as "Who am I?" and the importance of having a story to tell – your story – about your faith. Because I deal with this elsewhere, I won't repeat myself here, except to say one thing:

It's About Relationship

If you want to affect children's values, become a **significant adult** in their lives. This takes us back to the developmental stages. To review: A significant adult spends time with the child, plays and works with the child, and listens to the child. It's all about relationship. A relationship with you, and a relationship with God.

As for the child's relationship with you, let's listen to David Kupelian once more. "Your being any way other than *genuinely virtuous* – not perfect, mind you, but honestly and diligently seeking to do the right thing at all times – will drive your children crazy. Here's how the craziness unfolds: Children deserve and desperately need firmness, patience, fairness, limits, kindness, insight and a good, non-hypocritical example. In other words, they need genuine parental love and guidance. If they don't get this, they will resent you. Even if you can't see it, even if they can't see it and deny it, they will resent you for failing to give them real love. And that resentment... makes children feel compelled to rebel against you, and against all authority, out of revenge for your having failed them."[6] While this statement is about parents, it occurs to me that we can apply it to the church as well. Has the church failed to give our children real love? Is that another factor in their abandonment of us – because we abandoned them?

As for the child's relationship with God: You cannot lead a child to somewhere you've never been. Jesus wants to be the bread of *your* life. He wants to be *your* living water. He wants to be *your* way, *your* truth, *your* life. So don't be content just to know *about* Him. Seek a relationship with Him. Pursue Him for yourself.

How do you get to know God? To answer that question, look at how you get to know other humans. You spend time with them. Converse with them. Listen to them. Work and play with them. That's "significant person" stuff.

Back to the original question: How do you get to know God? Spend time with God. Talk with God. Listen to God. Work and play with God. Spending time with God is often called prayer. I'm talking about more than bow your head, close your eyes, and speak to God. I'm talking about a heart attitude of connection and relationship, an awareness of God's constant presence, and communication, sometimes formal, but mostly informal.

"Real prayer comes not from gritting our teeth but from falling in love." Richard Foster

"Prayer is doing business with God." Vi rginia Whitman

"Prayer means that we have come boldly into the throne room and we are standing in God's presence."
E.W. Kenyon

"I like to think of prayer as a conversation between two friends who love and understand each other. Prayer is the key that opens the door to a whole new world."

Hope MacDonald

"Prayer is the key that unlocks all the storehouses of God's... grace and power."

R.A. Torrey

"Prayer unites the soul to God."   Juliana of Norwich

"Oh, this thing of keeping in constant touch with God, of making him the object of my thought and the companion of my conversations, is the most amazing thing I ever ran across."

Frank Laubach

"True, whole prayer is nothing but love."   Augustine

"...prayer is not so much a way to find God as a way of resting in him... who loves us, who is near to us."

Thomas Merton

"Prayer makes a difference in what happens."
Randy Hatchett

"We can read all the books that have ever been written about prayer, but until we actually choose... to pray, we will never learn."

Hope MacDonald[7]

Needless to say, I think if we want to lead children to a living relationship with God, we must teach them about prayer and encourage them to pray. They cannot catch a relationship with God by osmosis. Only when they meet God and know Him can they have a lasting relationship with Him. But we can help position them and give them opportunity to meet Him.[8]

Support and Strength

Teaching is time-consuming and energy-consuming. Paul says he worked, "struggling with all (God's) energy, which so powerfully works in me" (Colossians 1:29). It's been said that God doesn't call the equipped, he equips the called. God doesn't give us a task to do and then not give us all we need to accomplish that task. But it's usually in the midst of a task that we find the strength. I dread weeding the garden, thinking of how tiring it's going to be. Then I get out among the plants and begin the task, and I find I can do it, sometimes a lot quicker than I had expected.

Hebrews 11 tells about people like Gideon, Samson, Samuel, and David "whose weakness was turned to strength" (Hebrews 11:32-34). We think of these people as strong. But they were just as weak as we are. They became strong when they let God use them for His purposes.

Have you ever watched geese fly? Each goose makes an "uplift" of air when it flaps its wings. This "uplift" helps the geese that are following. So when the whole flock flies in its "V" formation, the geese have 71% greater flying range than if each goose flew by itself. If a goose falls out of formation, it feels the drag of the resistant air and soon joins the flock again. When the lead goose gets tired, it leaves the front and moves back. Another goose takes its place. I'm sure you already see the analogy. Geese teach us about working as a team. There's an old saying, "Many hands make light work."

There's something else that's interesting about geese. The ones that are farther back in the formation honk to encourage the lead goose to keep moving. And if a goose gets sick or wounded, two others leave the flock to follow it down. They try to help and protect the hurting goose. They'll stay with the hurt goose until it dies or can fly again. Then they'll fly out with another flock of geese or catch up with their own flock. Paul wrote, "Encourage one another and build each other up... encourage the timid, help the weak, be patient with everyone..." (I Thessalonians 5:11, 14).

Peter was part of Jesus' close-knit "flock." He got to do something no one else had ever done. He got to walk on water. As long as he was looking at Jesus, he was fine. When he stopped looking at Jesus, he began to sink. I, too, find I get discouraged when I focus on my inadequacies and on the world around me instead of on Jesus. "Let us fix our eyes on Jesus, the author and perfecter of our faith... Consider him... so that you will not grow weary and lose heart" (Hebrews 12:2-3). I must remember that God is not joining my work. I am joining His. I am not in charge. He is. I have to keep my focus on Him.

To help us focus on God, I think we should read the eighth chapter of Romans at least once a month. There, Paul reminds us that we have no reason to ever have another bad day the rest of our lives. The chapter starts out saying, "Therefore, there is now no condemnation . . ." *There is no such thing as condemnation.* If we are in Jesus, condemnation is not even in our vocabulary. Here are some other highlights:

> "For you did not receive a spirit that makes you a slave again to fear, but you received the Spirit of sonship. And by him we cry, 'Abba, Father.'"

> "I consider that our present sufferings are not worth comparing with the glory that will be revealed in us."

> "The Spirit himself intercedes for us with groans that words cannot express."

> "We know that in all things God works for the good of those who love him..."

> "If God is for us, who can be against us?"

> "We are more than conquerors through him who loved us."

> "For I am convinced that neither death nor life, neither angels nor demons, neither the present nor the future, nor any powers, neither height nor depth, nor anything else in all creation, will be able to separate us from the love of God that is in Christ Jesus our Lord."

God offers us unchanging grace, unfailing love and undeniable mercies. The only thing that can get in the way is an unyielding heart.

Your Turn

When my niece was a preschooler, she asked her daddy, "When you die, do you go into the Bible?" She knew the Bible told stories of God's people who were no longer alive. She thought maybe our stories went in there too.

Bible stories give us glimpses of a magnificent time line. From Adam to Noah to Abraham, Isaac and Jacob. From Moses to David to Daniel. From Mary and Joseph to Peter, Paul and the apostle John. Picture this same time line running through history up to our time today. It is our privilege to be part of this ancient heritage and the story that continues to be woven.

You and I stand on a section of the Time Line that is post-modern, global, and pluralistic. Sometimes that's exciting. Sometimes it's discouraging. But "He (God) will be the sure foundation for your times" (Isaiah 33:6), whatever those times may be.

Each of us, being unique, fills a unique place on the time line. Your place is no less important than the place Joseph filled, or the place that David or Daniel or Ruth or Dorcas or Lydia stood in. You, in all your God-given uniqueness, are important, which means your unique contribution to the specific children and youth in your life is important.

There was once an old Hasidic Jewish leader named Zusia. He had many followers. One morning when Zusia joined his followers, they saw that his eyes were red and swollen as if he'd been crying.

"Zusia," they said. "What is wrong?"

Zusia wailed. "I have learned what the angels will ask me one day."

His followers were amazed that any question put to their beloved leader could be so disturbing. "What will they ask you?" said his followers.

"I have learned," said Zusia, "that the angels will not ask me, 'Zusia, why have you not been a Moses, leading your people out of their Egypt?'"

Again Zusia's followers were puzzled. "So what will the angels ask you?" they said.

"I have learned," said Zusia, "that the angels will not ask me, 'Zusia, why have you not been a Joshua, leading your people into their promised land?'"

Zusia's followers were even more curious. "So what will the angels ask you?" they said.

"I have learned," wailed Zusia, "that the angels will one day ask me, 'Zusia, why have you not been Zusia?'"

You have a place. You are unique and significant. Commit yourself, and keep your eyes on Jesus. I hope you, like Peter, have stepped out of the boat. The question now is: Will you watch Jesus or the waves?

> May God "equip you with everything good for doing His will, and may He work in us what is pleasing to Him, through Jesus Christ to whom be glory, for ever and ever. Amen."
>
> (Hebrews 13:21)

Notes

Chapter 1

1. David Elkind, *The Hurried Child* (Reading, MA: Addison, 1981).
2. C.D. Wright, "The Choice for Poetry," *The Writer*, May 1993.
3. *Zillions*, October/November 1993
4. Robert Coles, "The Man Who Listens to Children," *Storytelling*, Fall 1992.

Chapter 2

1. <http://www.medscape.com/medline/abstract/103499727> 18 September 2008. see also
<http://kidshealth.org/parent/emotions/feelings/anxiety.html> 18 September 2008.

Chapter 3

1. Robert Coles, *The Spiritual Life of Children* (Boston: Houghton, 1990).
2. John W. Santrock, *Life-Span Development* (Dubuque, IA: Brown, 1989).
3. James W. Fowler, *Stages of Faith: The Psychology of Human Development and the Quest for Meaning* (San Francisco: Harper, 1981).
4. Ibid.
5. Thomas Lickona, PH.D., *Raising Good Children* (New York: Bantam, 1983).
6. William Sears, M.D. and Martha Sears, R.N., *The Discipline Book* (Boston: Little, 1995).
7. Dorothy G. Singer and Tracey A. Revenson, *A Piaget Primer: How a Child Thinks* (New York: Penguin, 1978).
8. Howard Gardner, *The Unschooled Mind* (New York: Harper, 1991).
9. *Children's Ministry Resource Bible* (Nashville: Nelson, 1993), 1140.

Chapter 5

1. Scott Spencer as interviewed by Terri Gross on *Fresh Air*, National Public Radio, March 19, 2008.
2. E. Mavis Heatherington and Ross D. Parke, *Child Psychology: A Contemporary Viewpoint* (Boston: McGraw, 1999).

Chapter 6

1) Robert Solomon, tape series *No Excuses: Existentialism and the Meaning of Life* (Chantilly, VA: Teaching Company, 2000).
2. Raymond and Dorothy Moore, *Home Grown Kids* (Waco, TX: Word Books Publisher, 1981).
3. As quoted by Jim Trelease, *The Read-Aloud Handbook* (New York: Penguin Books, 1985).

Chapter 7

1. Chip Wood, *Yardsticks* (Greenfield, MA: Northeast Foundation for Children, 1994).
2. Stephen Jones, *Faith Shaping* (Valley Forge, PA: Judson Press, 1987)
3. Howard Gardner, *The Unschooled Mind* (New York: HarperCollins Publishers, 1991).

Chapter 8

1. Chip Wood, *Yardsticks*.
2. Juliet Schor, *Born to Buy* (New York: Scribner, 2004).
3. Ibid.
4. "Pluralism," <u>Merriam-Webster's Collegiate Dictionary</u>, eleventh ed., 2004.
5. Dick Crider, "Catch 'Em at the Back Door: Ministering to Preteens." Children's Ministry Leadership Conference, Calvary Chapel Conference Center, Murrieta, CA. March 6-8, 2006.
6. Daniel Goleman, interview in *What We Believe But Cannot Prove*, ed. John Brockman (New York: Harper, 2006).
7. Dick Crider, "Catch 'Em at the Back Door: Ministering to Preteens."
8. Jennifer Weinblatt, "Why I Love Your Middle Schooler," parentworld.com, October 2006.

Chapter 9

1. Chip Wood, *Yardsticks*.
2. Ron Habermas and David Olshine. *How to Have a Real Conversation with Your Teen* (Cincinnati: Standard, 1998).
3. "The Merchants of Cool" <www.pbs.org/wgbh/pages/frontline/shows/cool/view> accessed 10/01/08.
4. David Kupelian, "Selling Sex and Corruption to Your Kids" <www.worldnetdaily.com/news/article.asp?ARTICLE_ID=36598> accessed 10/01/08.
5. As quoted in "Teens Give Out MySpace Pages..." *USA Today*, Monday, January 9, 2006.
6. Kevin Huggins, *Parenting Adolescents* (Colorado Springs: Navpress, 1989).
7. Ibid.
8. Orson Scott Card, *Speaker for the Dead* (New York: Tor, 1991).
9. Kelly Bingham, "Facing Life Head On: Teen Protagonists," lecture at Southern Festival of Books, Nashville, TN, Fall 2008.
10. Orson Scott Card.
11. Ralph D. Winter, editorial, *Mission Frontiers*, September-October 2008. See also <www.therebelution.com/about/rebelution.htm> accessed 09/29/08.

Chapter 10

1. Dr. Brad Widstrom, The Amazing Race Seminar (Denver, April 2005).

Chapter 11

1. Bert Decker, *The Art of Communication* (Los Altos, CA: Crisp, 1988). See also: B. Boylan, *What's Your Point?* (New York: Warner, 1988).
2. Robert Coles, "The Man Who Listens to Children," *Storytelling*, Fall 1992.
3. Dr. Robert Hemfelt and Dr. Paul Warren, *Kids Who Carry Our Pain* (Nashville: Nelson, 1990).
4) Laura Ingalls Wilder, *On the Banks of Plum Creek* (New York: Harper, 1937).
5) As quoted by Vernie Schorr, *Building Relations with Children* (International Center for Learning, 1978).

Chapter 12

1. Dr. Rita Dunn and Dr. Kenneth Dunn, *Teaching Elementary Students through Their Individual Learning Styles* (Boston: Allyn, 1992).
2. Marlene D. LeFever, *Learning Styles* (Colorado Springs: Cook, 1995).
3. Ibid.
4. Ibid.
5. Ibid.
6. Thomas Armstrong, *7 Kinds of Smart* (New York: Penguin, 1993).
7. See also: Don Oldenburg, "A Hunger to Learn," *This World*, September 20, 1987.
8. Richard Lavoie. *The Motivation Breakthrough* (New York: Simon & Schuster, 2007).

Chapter 14

1. George Gerbner, Speech. 1990 National Congress on Storytelling.
2. Jim Trelease, *The Read-Aloud Handbook* (New York: Penguin, 1985)
3. Howard G. Hendricks, *The 7 Laws of the Teacher* (Atlanta: Walk Through the Bible Ministries, 1987).
4. Robert Coles, "The Man Who Listens to Children," *Storytelling*, Fall 1992.
5. Peninnah Schram, "Recalling Our Life Stories," *Yarnspinner*, February 1990.
6. Jack Maguire, *Creative Storytelling* (New York: McGraw, 1985).

Chapter 15

1. Mem Fox, *Wilfrid Gordon McDonald Partridge* (Brooklyn: Kane/Miller, 1984).
2. Frank Smith, *Insult to Intelligence* (Portsmouth, NH: Heinemann, 1988).

Chapter 16

1. William Sears, M.D. and Martha Sears, R.N., *The Discipline Book* (Boston: Little, 1995).
2. Grace Mitchell, *A Very Practical Guide to Discipline with Young Children* (Chelsea, MA: Telshare, 1982).
3. Bill Slonecker, M.D. Speech. 1993 Children's Pastors' Conference, Nashville, TN.
4. Grace Mitchell, *A Very Practical Guide to Discipline with Young Children.*
5. Don and Jeanne Elium, *Raising a Son: Parents and the Making of a Healthy Man* (Hillsboro, OR: Beyond Words, 1992).

Chapter 17

1. Ross Campbell, M.D., *Relational Parenting* (Chicago: Moody, 2000).
2. L. Tobin, *What Do You Do With a Child Like This?* (Duluth, MN: Whole Person, 1991).
3. Dr. Becky A. Bailey, *Conscious Discipline* (Oviedo, FL: Loving Guidance, 2000).
4. Dr. Robert Hemfelt and Dr. Paul Warren, *Kids Who Carry Our Pain* (Nashville: Nelson, 1990).
5. Richard Lavoie, *The Motivation Breakthrough.*

Chapter 18

1. Richard Lavoie, *The Motivation Breakthrough.*
2. David Kupelian, "Why Today's Youth Culture Has Gone Insane" <www.worldnetdaily.com/news/article.asp?ARTICLE_ID=36599> accessed 10/01/08.
3. John W. Santrock, *Life-Span Development* (Dubuque, Iowa: Wm. C. Brown Publishers, 1989).
4. James W. Fowler, *Stages of Faith: The Psychology of Human Development and the Quest for Meaning.*
5. For a 13-week curriculum teaching kids, ages eight through eleven, about other religions and why Jesus is the Way, see *Bridge-Quest: Why I Believe in Jesus* at KarynHenley.com.
6. David Kupelian, "Why Today's Youth Culture Has Gone Insane."
7. Quotes on prayer:
   > Foster - *Prayer: Finding the Heart's True Home,* by Foster, HarperCollins.
   > Whitman - *Change the World School of Prayer* manual, World Literature Crusade.
   > Kenyon - Ibid.
   > MacDonald - Ibid.
   > Juliana of Norwich - *Prayer: Finding the Heart's True Home,* by Foster, HarperCollins.
   > Laubach - Ibid.

Augustine - Ibid.

Merton - *Streams of Living Water,* by Richard J. Foster, HarperCollins.

Hatchett - *Holman Bible Dictionary*, Holman Bible Publishers.

MacDonald - *Change the World School of Prayer* manual, World Literature Crusade.

8. For a 13-week curriculum teaching kids, ages eight through eleven, how to pray, see *Prayer* at KarynHenley.com.

Visit us at **www.KarynHenley.com**
or call toll-free **1-888-573-3953** (U.S.)

- To learn about books, DVDs, music products and other resources by Karyn Henley.

- To request a FREE Karyn Henley catalog

- To sign up for Karyn's monthly newsletter

- To learn more about hosting a Karyn Henley Seminar at your church or school.